About the author

Peter Uvin is the Henry J. Leir Professor of International Humanitarian Studies and Academic Dean at the Fletcher School, Tufts University, USA. In recent years, his research and practice have dealt with the intersection between development aid, human rights, and conflict, mostly in the African Great Lakes region. His previous books include *Development and Human Rights* and *Aiding Violence: The Development Enterprise in Rwanda*, which received the African Studies Association's Herskowits award for the most outstanding book on Africa in 1998. He spends a large amount of his time working for various agencies in the Great Lakes region.

African Arguments

African Arguments is a series of short books about Africa today. Aimed at the growing number of students and general readers who want to know more about the continent, these books highlight many of the longer-term strategic as well as immediate political issues confronting the African continent. They get to the heart of why Africa is the way it is and how it is changing. The books are scholarly but engaged, substantive as well as topical.

Series editors

Titles already published

Forthcoming

William Gumede, *The Democracy Gap: Africa's Wasted Years*

Camilla Toulmin, *Climate Change in Africa*

Published by Zed Books and the IAI with the support of the following organizations:

InterAfrica Group The InterAfrica Group is the regional centre for dialogue on issues of development, democracy, conflict resolution and humanitarianism in the Horn of Africa. It was founded in 1988 and is based in Addis Ababa, with programmes supporting democracy in Ethiopia and partnership with the African Union and IGAD. <www.sas. upenn.edu/African_Studies/ Hornet/menu_Intr_Afr.html>

International African Institute The International African Institute's principal aim is to promote scholarly understanding of Africa, notably its changing societies, cultures and languages. Founded in 1926 and based in London, it supports a range of seminars and publications including the journal *Africa*. <www.internationalafricaninstitute.org>

Justice Africa Justice Africa initiates and supports African civil society activities in support of peace, justice and democracy in Africa. Founded in 1999, it has a range of activities relating to peace in the Horn of Africa, HIV/AIDS and democracy, and the African Union. <www.justiceafrica.org>

Royal African Society Now more than a hundred years old, the Royal African Society today is Britain's leading organization promoting Africa's cause. Through its journal, *African Affairs*, and by organizing meetings, discussions and other activities, the society strengthens links between Africa and Britain and encourages understanding of Africa and its relations with the rest of the world. <www.royalafricansociety.org>

Social Science Research Council The Social Science Research Council brings much-needed expert knowledge to public issues. Founded in 1923 and based in New York, it brings together researchers, practitioners and policymakers in every continent. <www.ssrc.org>

PETER UVIN

Life after violence
A people's story of Burundi

Zed Books

LONDON | NEW YORK

in association with

International African Institute
Royal African Society
Social Science Research Council

Life after violence: A people's story of Burundi was first published in association with the International African Institute, the Royal African Society and the Social Science Research Council in 2009 by Zed Books Ltd, 7 Cynthia Street, London N1 9JF, UK and Room 400, 175 Fifth Avenue, New York, NY 10010, USA

www.zedbooks.co.uk
www.internationalafricaninstitute.org
www.royalafricansociety.org
www.ssrc.org

Cover designed by Rogue Four Design
Set in OurType Arnhem and Futura Bold by Ewan Smith, London
index: <ed.emery@thefreeuniversity.net>
Printed and bound in Malta by Gutenberg Press Ltd

Distributed in the USA exclusively by Palgrave Macmillan, a division of St Martin's Press, LLC, 175 Fifth Avenue, New York, NY 10010.

A catalogue record for this book is available from the British Library
Library of Congress Cataloguing in Publication Data available

ISBN 978 1 84813 179 8 hb
ISBN 978 1 84813 180 4 pb
ISBN 978 1 84813 181 1 eb

Contents

Tables

Foreword

Burundi was the first country in Africa I set foot in. I still recall my first impressions, in 1985 – the heat and the humidity; the seriousness of the faces and the deep sense of humor of Burundians; the perfect combination of brochettes, fries, and Primus beer; my first taste of *ndagala* (small, salted fried fish) at the Cercle Nautique; the beauty of the men and women, and the ugly scars poverty inflicted on them. Over the years, I went there tens of times, to work in development projects, to do research, to advise agencies, to evaluate projects. I saw friends' children grow up, and heard about other friends who died, fled, married. The civil war intervened, and this poor country became poorer still, and sadder, and more afraid. The smiles disappeared, the scars were more common.

At about the same time, I married, moved continents, and stopped working for the development business. The genocide in Rwanda happened, less than a year after the sad reversal of democracy in Burundi and the outbreak of civil war there, and I was sick of the inefficiency, the blindness, the self-centeredness of the development business of which I had been a junior member until then.

I ended up writing a book, *Aiding Violence*, which was based on a detailed study of Rwanda but was equally inspired by my experiences in Burundi. This book came at a propitious time, when people everywhere were beginning to rethink their 'normal professionalism' of development and humanitarianism. Many changes have occurred since: rights-based approaches, conflict-sensitive development, and so on. I became a player in these changes, consulting about them on the ground, first in Rwanda and then in Burundi, and writing about them in policy and scholarly documents. These were heady times, with fascinating mandates, long discussions, and a feeling that we were building something new.

My previous book, *Human Rights and Development*, explores some of this.

In the meantime, I slowly and unexpectedly made a career in the academic world and became a professor. In 2006/07, I got a sabbatical, and decided it was time to go back to the source: the people of Burundi, where I had started. I wanted to know the ideas of the international development and peace-building community (of which I had been a more or less enthusiastic cog), the aims it seeks, the agendas it sets: do they make sense to regular people? Do Burundians talk about the same things as I do, even if they use different words? Or are people like me and my international colleagues, and the ideas/ideologies we represent, basically living in a totally different world, unrelated to the real lives of the poor and the excluded in whose names we claim to speak?

At that point in time, I was lucky enough to run into Maria Correia of the World Bank. She encouraged me to do this research, and found funding for it. She and her colleague Pia Peeters provided me not only with funding but also with major intellectual support, including a new focus I would not have attempted by myself: a focus on youth, masculinity, and conflict. Indeed, in my years of working in Africa, I rarely met or seriously talked to young people, and I surely never paid particular attention to how they view the future. I talked to a good friend and colleague of mine, Marc Sommers, who knows a lot more than I do about youth in that part of the world, and he enthusiastically encouraged me. I am grateful he did: without him and Maria Correia I would have missed out on the great conversations I had with young men and women in Burundi, and I would never have learned what I did. I am also profoundly grateful to the World Bank for its financial support of this research.

I was fortunate enough that the Simon Guggenheim Foundation awarded me a fellowship the same year: this was very important in helping me defray the many remaining costs of a year living far away, without other income, and with many unforeseen research and living expenses. Without this support, I would have had to end this project much sooner.

CARE-Burundi, finally, and its great director, Kassie McIlvaine, assisted me logistically in Burundi and provided a comfortable place to go to when I got lost.

Many people helped in writing this book, and foremost among them the many Burundians who gave me their time, their energy, intelligence, and humor: I hope this book does justice to them all. Kim Howe was a true friend and intellectual partner in both Burundi and the USA. Burundian friends such as Adrien Tuyaga, Benoit Birutegusa, and Pie Ngendakumana devoted hours and hours to me, giving me all their honesty and intelligence: what great friends you all are! My wife, Susan Cu-Uvin, let me go and live in Burundi for eight months in 2006, never once complaining, taking care of the household while having a full-time job herself. Heartfelt thanks to her.

Finally, the dedication. It is common to demonstrate one's impeccable taste and political correctness by dedicating a book to either local heroes or one's immediate family. I will depart from this path, and dedicate this book to a group of foreigners, all part of the much-maligned international development enterprise. They are all women who work in Burundi and whom I admire for their strength, their humanity, their real contributions to the country.

This book is dedicated, then, to

Kassie McIlvaine, country director of CARE-Burundi
Leanne Bayer, chief of party for PADCO-Burundi
Jill Morris, manager of PADCO's CBLP project
Liz McClintock, director of BLTP

Introduction

Burundi has arrived at a crossroads. A long history of conflict, ethnic polarization and politicization, authoritarian rule, a decade of civil war, and growing impoverishment lies on one side, and power-sharing arrangements, democratic elections, peace agreements, demobilization, and an infusion of development aid on the other. In between lies a generation of young people raised during a brutal war – years of education lost, hearts traumatized, and possessions lost. Some have fought, some have fled, some have stayed, but all have faced dramatically limited opportunities. These young adults who came of age during the war now represent the future of Burundi. But until now, there have been few if any attempts to accurately understand them.

The following pages present a snapshot of life as lived and analyzed by ordinary Burundians. This book is based on the voices of people – primarily young people – throughout Burundi: people who have been refugees, internally displaced, dispersed, ex-combatants; in the city and the *collines*, Hutu and Tutsi.

We set out to answer many questions. How are youth faring in post-conflict Burundi? Do young men pose a risk of renewed fighting and conflict? What does peace mean to them? How do they see socio-economic progress taking place in their own lives? How do gender norms and expectations influence their behavior and how have these norms changed as a result of the conflict? What do youth perceive to be their opportunities for the future? How is this different between ex-combatants and those who never fought? How do they relate to the state and development programs? What do they identify as their primary needs? How can internal and external organizations respond to their needs to help reduce the potential for violence in the future? The following report provides people's answers to all of these questions.

1

Chapters 1 and 2 provide the background: they present the methodology used and a brief political history of Burundi up to the time of our research. Chapters 3 to 7 present the results: they synthesize, and interpret, what ordinary Burundians told us about their definition of peace and war, their understanding of governance, their strategies for development, as well as gendered expectations of life. The last chapter synthesizes key insights, teasing out the implications of this work for the broader post-conflict, peace-building, and development literatures and for the policies of international agencies.

Definitions of youth vary dramatically. UNICEF defines it as twelve to twenty-five years old; Burundian law declares people to be adults at eighteen; in a conversation with the director-general of the Ministry of Youth, he set the age limit at thirty-five; and many ordinary Burundians, finally, define youth as being un-married (although others differed with that, arguing that more is required than simple marriage – responsible adult behavior is the key). When designing the research, we operationalized youth as people aged fifteen to thirty – the time during which a young person typically ends his or her studies, enters the work market, and establishes a family.

One more word. Fundamentally, the lives most of the people we interviewed lead are an affront to human dignity and totally deny any notion that there is an international community that stands for any values of equity or justice. The Burundians we met lived lives of stunning deprivation. Most of them never see any international aid. They die from easily preventable or curable diseases – tetanus, malaria – at scandalous rates. They work, or seek work, for endless hours, and go to sleep tortured by the cries of their hungry babies. The women and girls who have been raped are not treated; the young men who desperately try to survive are not helped; the local heroes who quietly fight for change are not recognized. The poverty of Burundi, and the stinginess of the international community when dealing with it, is revolting in our world of over-consumption.

Yet this is not how this book will feel. Speaking to Burundians, what emerged over and over is their quiet determination to improve their fates, their hope that the right things will be done, their dreams for personal and social change – and, frequently too, their condemnation of their fellow man, their desire to forget the past, their anger at the present.

PART ONE
Background

1 | A brief political history of Burundi

The pre-colonial period

Before the arrival of the colonizer, Burundi was a kingdom with a fine socio-political hierarchy. At the top, the king (Mwami) was surrounded by an aristocratic/princely class (Ganwa), which was in competition for the next kingship. The king was neither Hutu nor Tutsi – he embodied the nation. In the middle, various levels of Tutsi existed – first those at the royal court in Muramvya, the Tutsi-Banyaruguru; below them the ordinary pastoralist Tutsi, mainly Tutsi-Hima. Below, there were the large masses of Hutu. All these groups were divided and united by lineage and clan and by the changing vagaries of closeness to the court. The Twa, few in number, were ill considered by all. Hutu chiefs existed at different levels, and some Hutu played major roles in the royal administration. Finally, there were the Bashingantahe – wise men, appointed by local communities themselves, acting as local mediators and judges. Many of them were Hutu. This is very similar to neighboring Rwanda, but Burundi's pre-colonial set-up was more inclusive, more stable, than Rwanda's.

What is similar to Rwanda is that there is in Burundi a lot of debate about the nature of key historical trends and concepts as well, starting with the very basic ones: are Hutu, Tutsi and Twa different races? Different ethnic groups, with different historical origins? Or simply different castes, socio-professional organizations that are rather closed off and hereditary but leave some measure of flexibility? Could people change from Hutu to Tutsi and vice versa? Was the king originally Hutu? And the Ganwa?

There were no wars or conflicts between Hutu and Tutsi during these years: this does not mean that equality prevailed or that stereotypes were absent – traditional proverbs clearly show that not to be the case – but that the system displayed a fair degree of legitimacy and was capable of addressing social conflicts.

The colonial period

Germany, briefly, and then Belgium, for four decades, controlled Burundi through indirect rule. The king and his court and administrators continued to run the country, with the colonial authority simply an extra layer on top. Serious reforms of the system were, however, undertaken by Belgium from 1926 to 1933. The Ganwas and Tutsis were seen by the colonial power as the ruling group while the Hutus were naturally destined to obey, and all Hutu authorities were dismissed. As a result, while formally the old political structure of the country remained intact, colonization profoundly altered its nature. Political, social, and economic relations became more rigid, unequal, and biased against Hutu. The power and wealth of the Ganwa particularly, as well as some Tutsi, increased (Prunier 1994). Higher education was rarely extended to the population, and the few who had access to it were, again, powerful Ganwa and Tutsi.

At the same time, the state intervened more heavily in people's lives. New taxes were introduced, as was mandatory cropping and occasional forced labor for the maintenance of streets and buildings. Some of these measures were ostensibly for the people's benefit – mandatory manioc cropping, for example, to reduce the risk of famine, or ditch digging to combat water-induced erosion. Others were needed by the colonial state to pay for its upkeep – mandatory coffee production to pay for taxes, for example. A deeply interventionist but low-capacity state that would turn independent on 1 July 1962 was created.

The first few years of independence

In 1958, a nationalist party, UPRONA (Union pour le Progrès National), had been founded by Prince Louis Rwagasore – a popular, modern, pro-independence son of a deposed king, with good links to the Hutu community. In a countermove, the

Belgian administration helped create the PDC (Parti Démocrate Chrétien), which was led by chiefs close to Belgium. The Ganwa split between the two parties. UPRONA dominated the 1961 legislative elections, gaining 58 of the 64 seats. The party was truly multi-ethnic: of those elected, 25 were Tutsi, 22 Hutu, 7 Ganwa, and 4 of mixed parentage. Prince Rwagasore was assassinated by agents of the PDC on 13 October 1961. The historic significance of Rwagasore's murder is enormous: it is truly a day on which doors were closed for Burundi. Note that all this took place against the backdrop of Rwanda's 'social revolution' (1959–62), in which the monarchy was overthrown, thousands of Tutsi lost their lives, and tens of thousands fled the country – including to Burundi. From now on, increasingly, the Rwandan term for *demokarasi*, referring to ethnic majority politics, would sound appealing to some Burundian Hutu and scary to most Tutsi (Chrétien 2000).

During the next four years, Burundian politics was extremely unstable and gridlocked. The main parties became divided internally, the Hutu–Tutsi division became much more important, government after government fell, extremist positions increased. A failed 1965 Hutu gendarmerie *coup d'état* led to exemplary retribution, with thousands dead – a pattern that would repeat itself many more times over the next decades. The Tutsi military officer in charge of repressing that operation, Major Michel Micombero, was soon offered a ministerial position in the government. A few months later, in a bloodless *coup d'état*, he took over the government and declared the First Republic, with himself as president.

This was the start of almost three decades of military rule by a small group of Tutsi-Hima from Bururi province: Michel Micombero (1966–76), Jean-Baptiste Bagaza (1976–87), and Pierre Buyoya (1987–93). Their rule constituted the creation of a low-caste Tutsi dictatorship.

Burundi was dominated by one party – UPRONA. With the party's women's and youth movement, all Burundians were theoretically members. There was little separation of power between executive, legislature, judiciary, the single party, and the army. The central clique derived its power from control over the higher echelons of the army, the key levers of the state (and, consequently, aid flows) and party, as well as the small business sector. Dissent was crushed increasingly violently.

The events of 1972 had a profound impact on Burundi's politics. After an uprising by Hutu and Congolese rebels, during which Tutsi were killed, the army went on a two-month pogrom, systematically killing all educated Hutu throughout the country. At the very least 80,000 were killed (but some estimates are much higher); many more fled the country. Hutu thereafter lived in fear of a repetition of what Lemarchand (1996) has called a 'selective genocide.'

In the following decades, Burundi developed a system of almost total exclusion of Hutu. By 1985, there were only 4 Hutu cabinet ministers (out of 20), 17 Hutu MPs (out of 65), and 2 Hutu members of UPRONA's Central Committee (out of 52). Only 1 out of 22 ambassadors was Hutu, and only 2 provincial governors out of 15. Hutu amounted only to 10 percent of the teachers and 20 percent of the students at the National University; 89 percent of public corporation managers were Tutsi. All 37 highest command positions within the army were Tutsi (of which 27 were from Bururi province) (Nkurunziza and Ngaruko 2002). Jackson (2000) notes that just one commune of Bururi province, Mugamba, accounted for 15 percent of the 6,000 students of the University of Burundi, and that in the late 1980s the government allocated about 60 percent of donor aid to education for Bururi. Given that the formal labor market is dominated by public employment and that access depends on education, these government policies meant that the large majority of the population was structurally excluded from advancing. Yet Burundi's form of apartheid went undiscussed in aid circles or international liberation politics.

The state became further centralized, imposing its controls in all domains of the country's social, political, and economic life. A plethora of state enterprises was created, allowing for clientelism in job distribution and graft of the proceeds. Corruption became widespread. Resources were drained; land was confiscated through various extralegal means; enormous profits were made by the use of monopolies with import and sales licenses. The state became primarily 'a milking cow' for the elites that controlled it (Gasana 2002; Nkurunziza and Ngaruko 2002).

This inefficient and unjust system came increasingly under attack. As the economy stalled and debts mounted, structural adjustment was imposed. Even though only partly implemented, it upset the system and increased political and economic competition among elites and aspiring elites. Internally, in late 1988, Hutu mobs, organized by the Parti pour la Libération du Peuple Hutu (PALIPEHUTU), a clandestine radical movement born in the Tanzanian refugee camps in 1972 and with bases in Rwanda, attacked local Tutsi in the northern communes of Ntega-Marangara (close to where I did my research). Hundreds of Tutsi were killed. The army answered with the usual indiscriminate massive reprisals. At about the same time, the international community – including, importantly, the French, who had provided the main international support for the regime – began talking seriously about democratization.

1993 elections and the beginning of the crisis

In the wake of this crisis, and recognizing the growing international and internal pressures, President Buyoya began a series of important reforms. He assigned twelve Hutu and twelve Tutsi to the National Commission to Study the Question of National Unity. A Charter of National Unity was subsequently ratified. He also created parity in government by assigning many Hutu to senior positions, including that of prime minister (to make sure, however, Buyoya retained the functions of president of the country and of the party as well as minister of defense; the key ministries of the interior, justice, and the police also remained under Tutsi control, and the entire army top brass remained mono-ethnically Tutsi, with devastating consequences). The atmosphere of inclusion led to the creation in 1992 of the country's first NGOs, two human rights organizations (SONERA, closely connected to the Tutsi cause, and League ITEKA, which came to be seen as associated with the Hutu cause). A new, multiparty constitution was drafted, with provisions that all parties should be multi-ethnic. The new system of cooptation seemed to be working.

Yet the 1993 elections took place in a climate of growing ethnic antagonism and radicalization. Prunier (1994) suggests that the events in Ntega-Marangara were deliberately provoked by hard-liners in the government and the army who wanted to undermine Buyoya's 'liberalizing intentions.' PALIPEHUTU, in turn, was only too glad to oblige, for it too feared it would lose its clout if successful change took place. PALIPEHUTU infiltrations and tracts spread; scary rumors of failed coups, killing plans, and militia were a daily affair. At the same time, the FPR[1] was recruiting people throughout the region, including in Burundi; it invaded Rwanda and started a brutal civil war there. The then Rwandan president Habyarimana, in turn, supported PALIPEHUTU. According to some, PALIPEHUTU cadres infiltrated the Front pour la Démocratie au Burundi (FRODEBU, a semi-clandestine organization that originated in 1990) at the local level, and they are responsible for the organized murder of thousands of Tutsi throughout the country after the failed *coup d'état* of October 1993.

The elections eventually mainly pitted Uprona against FRODEBU, with both parties clearly identified along ethnic lines, even though they were theoretically bi-ethnic (Reyntjens 1995). The 1 June 1993 presidential elections were won by Melchior Ndadaye, the FRODEBU candidate, who received 64.75 percent of the vote, while Buyoya received 32.39 percent. The FRODEBU victory in parliament was even greater. In ethnic terms parliament comprised 85 percent Hutu and 15 percent Tutsi representatives, closely paralleling the supposed ethnic make-up of the country.

Ndadaye took the same cooperative line as Buyoya, appointing several Tutsi to cabinet positions, including as prime minister. Forty percent of the ministers in the new government came from other parties. At lower levels, however, FRODEBU held more posts: all the governors were replaced, with fourteen out of the new sixteen being from FRODEBU. This tendency also existed at communal levels.

After 100 days in power, President Ndadaye, as well as the president and vice-president of the National Assembly (i.e. the full constitutionally described succession), were killed in a *coup d'état*. It is generally believed that this coup was the counter-reaction to the rapid 'FRODEBU-ization' of the middle and lower levels of the state (many Tutsi and UPRONA loyalists lost their jobs in these weeks), and the fear that the army, the prime tool of protection of the Tutsi, would soon follow. The coup itself formally failed a few days later, after an international outcry, bolstered by freezes of aid. Yet the dynamics it had set in motion remained: a constitutional crisis that was to last for years, mass violence throughout the country, and further confirmation for both sides that the other was not to be trusted.

Thousands of Tutsi were killed in the hills in the days after the coup. Prunier writes that

> the first violent acts appear to have been spontaneous and to have been triggered by the news of President Ndadaye's arrest and death. But quickly FRODEBU local cadres 'organized the resistance,' an ambiguous term since in the first days nobody attacked them. In fact, they organized the indiscriminate massacre of ordinary Tutsi peasants who were collectively scapegoated for the murder of the President. Pro-UPRONA Hutu were also massacred along with Tutsi as they were considered 'accomplices' of the 'UPRONA coup.' Two days later, when the Army moved to stop these killings, it immediately started its own indiscriminate killings of Hutu.

Another specialist, Reyntjens (1995: 16), disagrees, seeing the killings of Tutsi as partly spontaneous popular anger and partly the act of some local FRODEBU politicians. He concludes that

13

'there is no evidence that a genocidal plan ever existed, and the allegations that it did were part of a strategy to exonerate the army and to implicate Frodebu.'

For thirty years, political competition in Burundi had become increasingly violent and ethnic in nature: now, the floodgates were open, and civil war had begun. As no side managed to acquire the upper hand, a decade of violence began. The civil war and ensuing genocide in neighboring Rwanda deepened the ethnic dimension. The year 1993 was the defining moment for many Tutsi, who feel that they were victims of a genocide that was only stopped by the (belated) intervention of the army.

A political stalemate followed, which UPRONA, as well as a slew of one-person radical Tutsi parties, used to work their way (back) into government, eventually coming to control the government far beyond what the election results warranted; in Reyntjens' (ibid.: 16) words, this 'creeping coup' consisted of 'the imposition of a de facto constitutional order which in effect consolidated the achievements of the coup.' After long negotiations, a new president was chosen in January 1994 – Cyprien Ntyamira (FRODEBU, Hutu). He was killed a few months later in the same plane crash that killed Rwandan president Habyarimana and marked the start of the genocide there.

More arduous negotiations followed, leading to a new convention in October 1994 that gave as many ministerial posts to UPRONA as to FRODEBU. The new government was riddled by infighting and conflict, and incapable of ruling: each side totally distrusted the other and saw its main function as sabotaging any plan of the other side. The country descended into terror. The city of Bujumbura continued to be rocked by extreme violence by mainly Tutsi but also Hutu militias. The years up to 1996 were years of absolute terror for people living in Bujumbura: no urban person has forgotten those terrible days.

In the summer of 1994, Léonard Nyangoma, until recently a FRODEBU interior minister and leader of a militia that controlled Kamenge (a neighborhood in Bujumbura we did part of our research in), took up arms, claiming his party had ceded too much power to UPRONA. This was the birth of the second major armed rebel movement, the Conseil National pour la Défense de la Démocratie (CNDD), after the Front National de Libération (FNL), the armed wing of the PALIPEHUTU. The CNDD eventually repeatedly split. At the end, one wing was led by Nyangoma (which participated in the 2005 elections as CNDD-Nyangoma), the other by Peter Nkurunziza, who would become Burundi's president, his party known under the original acronym of CNDD/FDD (Forces de Défense de la Démocratie). It is estimated that the FDD had about 18,000 soldiers and the FNL 5,000.

The war and the negotiations

Hutu rebel groups emerged, split, and launched attacks from Tanzania and the Democratic Republic of Congo. The political process was deadlocked. Presidents came and went. Chaos reigned. Violence prevailed. The city of Bujumbura became ethnically cleansed: Tutsis and Hutus lived in separate worlds, cut off from each other. Crossing into a zone of another ethnicity meant risking your life. Thousands fled their homes, either to safer havens around communal headquarters and military garrisons (mainly Tutsis, as they felt safer near the army and the police); or to the hills far from the army; or to neighboring countries, notably Tanzania. Tutsis were summarily executed by the FDD. Hutus were forcibly rounded up by the FAB (Forces Armées Burundaises) in '*camps de regroupement*' without food and safety. The FNL fired shells indiscriminately from the hills around Bujumbura. Around 300,000 people were killed in Burundi, over 500,000 refugees fled, and another 800,000 were displaced internally, often for many years.

In July 1996, Buyoya launched a second coup, presumably aimed at stabilizing the situation and avoiding a possible international military intervention. A regional embargo was immediately imposed, and years of further fighting, negotiation, and economic impoverishment followed.

The international community from early on sought a negotiated solution to the crisis. The USA, the EU, South Africa,

Tanzania, the OAU, and the neighboring heads of state all played major roles in these negotiations. Ten summits were held between June 1996 and August 2000 alone. Under enormous international pressure, including some last-minute arm-twisting by South Africa, the Arusha Peace and Reconciliation Agreement was eventually signed on 28 August 2000 (Chrétien 2000; ICG 2004). This agreement and its protocols marked the beginning of the transition out of war toward the development of new institutions designed to support and maintain peace, integrate the army, adopt a new constitution, organize elections, and kick-start development – a tall agenda.

While the Arusha agreement started by saying that the conflict in Burundi was 'fundamentally political, with extremely important ethnic dimensions; it stems from a struggle by the political class to accede to and/or remain in power,'[2] it went on to deal mainly with the ethnic issue. The most relevant sections for our purposes are in Protocol II, entitled 'Democracy and Good Governance,' which stipulates that:

- There will be two vice-presidents from different political parties and ethnic groups.
- The government will contain 60% Hutu and 40% Tutsi.
- The same proportion holds in Parliament. In addition, there will be a minimum of 30% women, and three Twa deputies will be coopted.
- No ethnic group may have more than 67% of the positions of communal administrator.
- Public enterprises shall have 60% Hutu and 40% Tutsi.

One of the most important stipulations of the Arusha agreement was the creation of a transitional government, with ministers from both the G7 (seven Hutu parties, including some big ones such as FRODEBU and CNDD[3]) and the G10 (ten Tutsi parties, all of them very small), and a Tutsi president (Buyoya) and Hutu vice-president (Ndayizeye) – with the former to leave his post after eighteen months to be replaced by the latter. President Buyoya kept his word and stepped down on 1 May 2003, which was a milestone in the transition and paved the way for the agreement with the CNDD/FDD.

But in the meantime the fighting continued unabated – indeed, most observers agree that there was more violence afterwards than before, for the main Hutu rebel movements had not been included in the Arusha negotiations. It took years more of fighting and negotiating until the largest Hutu rebel movement, the CNDD/FDD, agreed to the Pretoria Protocol on Political, Defense, and Security Power-sharing in Burundi (October 2003). This paved the way for their integration into the institutions of the state and the army. And it was only in September 2006 that a similar agreement was signed (this time by the CNDD/FDD-dominated elected government) with the FNL. As of this writing, however, this agreement has still not been implemented.

From the transition period to the elections

Even after the signing of the agreements, the remaining military, political, economic, and socio-psychological challenges were enormous. Many feared the peace process would not hold.

The security situation needed to be stabilized. Soldiers and rebels had to lay down their arms, some to be integrated into the national army and others demobilized and reintegrated into their communities. Rebels who had not signed the agreements had to be brought into the fold; police and army structures needed to be reformed and personnel trained, their leadership and 'rank and file' to become more multi-ethnic.

A viable system of guarantees had to be created to ensure that ethnic exclusion and destruction would not reoccur. While the initial conflict was clearly rooted in the competition for political power, ethnicity had in the last thirty years – and especially the last decade – taken on a life of its own. The social and physical separation between people had grown, and a sense of victimization prevailed (the charge of genocide being the trump card on both sides). The power-sharing arrangements in the Arusha accord were responses to that but would not work without popular support.

A brief political history

The old clique controlling power had to be persuaded to withdraw from control of the state, army, and economy. New arrivals had to be included in these spheres of power. In the immediate post-Arusha phase, this process was managed in part by a temporary expansion of the number of elite positions available, especially in the realm of the state: a large number of well-paid ministers and parliamentarians allowed most of the competitors for state power to find a safe haven for a few years. In Burundi, as in so many extremely poor African countries with almost no private sector, ceasing to be a general, a parliamentarian, or a minister is not simply a move to another interesting and well-paid job, but risks a complete loss of economic security and a fall from social grace. For at least some of Burundi's leaders, justice would lead them to face prosecution; elections would make them lose their positions of influence; security-sector reform and demobilization would make them lose jobs; good governance would reduce their income, etc.

Institutional transformation had to be achieved against a backdrop of unimaginable poverty and the social exclusion of most Burundians. The rural and urban poor, whether Hutu, Tutsi, or Twa, were the ones being killed and abused by all sides. They were the ones whose land was stolen, whose food, credit, and aid were being skimmed off, whose children were dying from preventable diseases at a rate that is one of the world's three highest. Few of those in power or vying for it, regardless of their party affiliation, were deeply connected to the poor or seemed to have their interests at heart. Apart from being unethical, this is a potentially risky situation in the longer term, as any political entrepreneur will find in Burundi's massive underclass an explosive reservoir of anger, cynicism, and potential violence.

There also existed, however, a number of contextual factors pushing in the direction of peace and institutional change. By 2003, most people were sick of an unwinnable war. A mutually hurting stalemate had prevailed for years by then – Reyntjens (1995: 21) already describes the situation in these terms in 1995 – and both sides knew that military victory was impossible. Grudgingly, but unavoidably, the politics of compromise took over.

At the same time, ordinary people of all ethnicities faced such hardship that they came to realize that ethnic division did not serve them. The size of the cake available has become much smaller for almost all Burundians: the economy is worse off than it was a decade ago – when it was already one of the world's poorest. This negatively affects both those in rural areas who live on the brink of starvation, and those in power, whose jobs are more precarious, their salaries lower, and the costs of living higher.

The Arusha agreement, warts and all, created incentives for collaboration and compromise, and provided a road map for the way ahead. The fact that ethnicity was becoming more openly addressed in society was real and positive. The media, stronger by the day, played a similar progressive role. The extremists on all sides were losing their capacity to derail the process. The constant engagement of the international community ensured that the process moved forward.

Probably the most crucial element of the transition was military integration and demobilization. The Pretoria agreement stipulated that at the level of the *état-major*, the FAB would have 60 percent and the CNDD-FDD 40 percent of the officers, while ethnic parity would prevail for the other commanding positions. But the detail was left to be resolved, including the timetable, harmonization of ranks, and even the definition of a combatant. After much wrangling, all this has been achieved in the newly integrated Forces de Défense Nationale (FDN). This integration is the cornerstone of the new Burundi: both sides control half the army and the police, and feel that they cannot be victimized by the other side. In the meantime, a real *esprit de corps* is developing in the army. Without this cooperation between military elites, supported by the international community, the transition would have failed (Vandeginste 2006); FAST (2005: 7) observes that there is a 'growing loyalty of the army to the new Hutu-dominated government. Even though the NDF appear to have committed serious human rights abuses in dealing with the NFL rebels, there is no evidence of ethnic prejudice, as was so obviously the case during the 1993 crisis.' This, precisely, is the basis of the new Burundi.

Besides these negotiations on integration there was the issue of disarmament, demobilization, and reintegration, which started late but made remarkable progress. To date, approximately 3,000 child soldiers, 21,000 FAB soldiers, 17,000 Gardiens de la Paix (youth defending their towns, supported by the former FAB), 26,041 rebel soldiers, and almost 9,000 Militants-Combattants (supporters of the rebels) have been demobilized.

The elections and after

A new constitution, based on the Arusha agreement, was approved by referendum on 28 February 2005. In June 2005, a four-phase electoral process began, all phases of which were won by CNDD/CFDD. Peter Nkurunziza was overwhelmingly elected president on 19 August 2005. The population massively voted *against* the parties that had been in power during the war (FRODEBU got 22 percent, against 71 percent in the previous elections; UPRONA, de facto in power for most of the last four decades, had 7 percent of the vote, half of its 1993 score) and in favor of the de facto winner, which had already established a strong network of local control throughout most of the country. There was also an element of regionalism, as some politicians, most notably Nyangoma in Bururi, scored significant victories in their home regions. The elections themselves took place in a period of relative calm. Some Tutsi politicians, looking to retain lucrative positions, defected to other parties – particularly to the CNDD/FDD. At the local level, human rights violations and significant intimidation took place as parties sought to control the vote.

UPRONA and MRC are the two predominantly Tutsi parties in parliament. Their seventeen deputies in the National Assembly are all Tutsi. The main Hutu parties are the CNDD/FDD, FRODEBU and the CNDD (Nyangoma). Approximately a quarter

TABLE 1.1 Election results, 2005

	Commune	National Assembly[2]		Senate
CNDD/FDD	1,781	59	64	32
FRODEBU	822	25	30	5
UPRONA	260	10	15	2
CNDD-Nyangoma	135	4	4	3
MRC-Rurenzangemero[1]	88	2	2	0
PARENA	75	0	0	0
Others	64	0	0	0
Ethnic Twa			3	3
Former presidents				4

Notes: 1. National Resistance Movement for the Rehabilitation of the Citizen. 2. The first figure under the National Assembly results represents the seats after the elections, and the second the final composition of the National Assembly after eighteen additional members were coopted in line with the Arusha agreement.

of the CNDD and FRODEBU deputies are Tutsi, as are a third of CNDD/FDD.

President Nkurunziza has adhered scrupulously to the constitutional requirements for ethnic and gender balance (Vandeginste 2006), and the appointment of General Niyoyankana as minister of defense was of major symbolical importance in appeasing Tutsi fears (FAST 2006).

The government clearly sees itself as a fresh break in Burundi's history: a government representing the majority of the people, inclusive and negotiated, and connected to the ordinary people in ways in which no previous government was. This is attested by the extremely high degree of outreach conducted by senior government people, foremost among them the president, who as an individual is connected to the rural masses the way no Burundian president has ever been. His first decision – free elementary schooling for all Burundians – exemplified this perfectly: in a country where social exclusion took place through highly unequal access to education, and in which the war had further destroyed the educational system, the decision constituted a radical and visible break with the past; our interviews showed this decision is deeply appreciated by ordinary people everywhere. The decision to provide free healthcare to pregnant women and children under five follows a similar pattern.

At the same time, there are other political dynamics at work. The core of the government comes out of a former military movement. In many other African countries (Rwanda, Eritrea, Ethiopia), this has led to a tendency toward authoritarian, top-down, non-consensual politics. This tendency clearly exists in Burundi as well: during my stay there, journalists, civil society leaders, and opposition politicians were frequently imprisoned under trumped-up charges. Much of the government is also rather inexperienced in managing a major bureaucracy, with all this implies in terms of contradictory messages, unclear policies, problems with the donor community, etc. They are not helped in this respect by the fact that the experienced senior civil servants in the bureaucracy belong to the two losing political parties and hence often do nothing to help the new government, rather enjoying seeing it fail. Finally, there are major divisions within the governing party, consuming much of its leadership's time, and leading to constant jockeying and protecting one's back. This came to a climax in late 2006 and early 2007, with the ouster of party president Husain Rajabu.

Synthesizing and looking ahead

The transition in Burundi can rightly be seen as a major success story for the international community – and one that is not known by anyone. Burundi is a country totally devoid of any importance: it has no economic or geo-strategic value to speak of. And yet, the international community has invested enormous amounts of time, energy and money in promoting a resolution of Burundi's violent conflict. It kept investing time and money for years, never giving up, bringing protagonists together, acting as intermediary, absorbing the costs of negotiations and implementation of the key provisions of the transition, taking real risks in the process. When international donors funded the cantonment camps for rebels – effectively housing and feeding rebels accused of gross human rights violations for as long as a year – this was a daring move, which paid off when they were either demobilized or integrated into the army or police.

This international community was a diversified group. It included the UN and a slew of foreign powers – the formal colonizer, Belgium; the former protector, France; the other usual major players in the region, the USA, the UK, and the EU – all of whom made enormous efforts to develop coordinated and coherent pro-peace policies for Burundi. They sent special envoys, created coordination mechanisms in their own capitals, and generally kept their eye on the prize. But a uniquely important role was also played by African countries. The regional heads of state (Tanzania, Uganda, Rwanda) met constantly and tried to speak with one voice to Burundians – something that has had a very strong impact, so different from the past, when neighbors could always be counted on to pour oil on the flames. The African Union sent in a peacekeeping force in 2003. South Africa's leadership in the transition was unparalleled, and continues up until today, as its diplomats try to finalize negotiations with the FNL.

The international community now also extends about $300 million per year in aid to Burundi – an increase since the lean years of the embargo and the aid freeze, but by no means very much money. An enormous proportion of this money goes into the superstructure: salaries and perks for experts, consultants, managers. Compared to the billions of dollars poured into Afghanistan, Iraq, or the former Yugoslavia, this is peanuts, although it is perfectly in line with what African countries generally receive after war. Compared to the size of the problems Burundi faces, it is a drop on a hot plate as well: if these were our own children, we would cry with pain. But these are Africans, and we do have good arguments against giving more: 'We' (the USA, the West, the willing, the international community – take your pick) did not destroy their country or create the conflict; more money does not buy peace (Iraq and Afghanistan are indeed good examples of that) or development (a more contentious argument, although widely accepted); they cannot spend more money in any case, for they lack the absorption capacity (not entirely untrue either). As it stands, the national budget for 2006 totals $417 million,[4] of which $341 million is externally financed – a whopping 82 percent (PBC 2006)! So I leave it up to the reader to decide whether this is too much, too little, or about right.

The fact is that Burundians have come to the end of a long road. The voyage has been painful beyond imagination. Nobody will bring back the people hacked to death; the innocence of the children raped; the lives of the youth who were burned alive, oil-doused tires around their necks; the small possessions families had gathered and passed on over generations that were stolen; the people pulled off buses and shot in the neck beside the road simply for being of the 'wrong' ethnic group. Nobody can restore the hearts, the minds, the bodies of so many Burundians whose eyes turn distant and tired when they remember the past – before they turn away from the subject, embarrassed and pained.

Burundians have faced their demons and come to another place. They have a functioning albeit weak democracy now, a free press, a vibrant civil society – far ahead in every respect of neighboring Rwanda. They have devised a system of cooptation and consociationalism that is uniquely theirs, and they have implemented it beyond what many thought was possible. The army is integrated, and everyone feels relieved by that. Hundreds of thousands of displaced people have returned home, although as many as 200,000 remain in camps. Similarly, hundreds of thousands of refugees have returned to Burundi, although, once again, many remain abroad. Not all is done yet, of course – how could it be? But everyone agrees that things are moving forward.

How do ordinary Burundians, in the hills and the ghettoes, look at life? What does peace mean to them? How do they relate to the state? How do they see socio-economic progress taking place in their own lives? What are their priorities? And what are the gender aspects of all this? It is to their insights into these matters that the rest of this book is devoted. But first we need a short chapter on methodology. Please stick with it – it is not as bad as you might fear, and really helpful to an understanding of the rest of the book.

A brief political history

2 | Methodology and location

Interviews

The prime source of information used in this research is 388 in-depth interviews with ordinary Burundians throughout the country. On average, these interviews were about two hours long. Most of them were conducted with individuals and with small groups of two to four people.

After a few weeks of working in Busiga, the town we started our research in, we abandoned the use of focus groups, because the sort of personal analysis and experience we sought to hear cannot easily emerge from such group conversations. From then on, we decided to interview only individuals, or very small groups of people who naturally and spontaneously fit together.

Our interviews were as unstructured, open-ended, and flexible as possible: we wanted to discuss certain issues, but we did not care in what order, nor did we necessarily always need to get them *all* discussed (although we did try to cover as much of the ground as possible). Michael Quinn Patton describes four levels of interviews, from 'informal conversation' (where the subject often does not even know s/he is being interviewed) to 'closed, fixed-response interviews' (basically questionnaires) (2002: 349). Our approach squarely falls into his second category, 'interview guide approach,' in which 'topics and issues to be covered are specified in advance, in outline form; the interviewer decides sequence and wording of questions in the course of the interview.' The interview schedule itself consisted of only twenty-one questions. All these questions sought to probe into people's perceptions, dreams, and analysis of development, governance, the future – *their future*.

We encouraged people to ask questions if they had any. In the rural areas, people systematically asked the same thing: *What are you going to do with this?* In urban areas, the questions were often more direct, sometimes a tad aggressive: *So, now that you've asked us all these questions, what's in it for you?* We very much enjoyed all these questions: they forced us to be honest with ourselves and with them, and they did help to equalize the playing field a bit. Sometimes people also asked us for our opinion about the questions we had posed them.

At times, when we had spent some time in a particular location and word had spread about our presence, people approached us for interviews. Surprisingly, these were often very poor or vulnerable people, typically women and frequently widows, who wanted someone to listen to their story, just for once. These were some of the most amazing conversations we had.

We felt strongly that the value of our research did not justify the risk of retraumatizing people, especially as we had nothing to offer in terms of services or support. As a result, we did not collect much information on painful private matters. For example, I am sure that household conflicts are one of the most serious problems faced by many Burundians, especially women and children. The stunning outside pressures Burundians have been subjected to – the ravages of war, the insecurities of banditry and theft, the grinding pressure of misery, the land scarcity and the fear for tomorrow – often get mediated into deep and long-lasting intra-household conflicts, pitting husbands against wives, brothers against sisters, children of one marriage against children of another. These conflicts are very painful and debilitating: they take up enormous energy, and create fear and pain in the lives of people who are already under considerable stress. Yet our conversations rarely addressed these issues. There were many allusions, but few direct discussions. Similarly, some ex-combatants and women hinted at personal war trauma, but few elaborated. So, clearly, our research did not get at some of the most painful and private things in people's lives. This was the price I was willing to pay in order not to push people into sensitive and painful territory, but it is a price that must be acknowledged.

Finally, for research like this, the quality of the translators is crucial. Kirundi is a language of allusion and proverbs: information is conveyed between the lines, hinted at, but rarely expressed directly. The challenge is also social: the translator is the front-line person who interacts with the interviewees, making the connection, maintaining the social aspects of the relation, putting people at ease.

I was fortunate to be able to hire excellent translators, with considerable experience. In rural areas, I worked with two young women, Etionette and Alice, who had lengthy experience in promoting rural dialogues. Their capacity to interact with people, put them at ease, listen with empathy and respect was crucial to the success of this research.

Midway through the research project, Alice left and I added Innocent, who was initially our driver. Every time we returned to the car at the end of the day, we found him hanging out with local youth, kicking a ball, chatting. After his 'promotion,' he ended up doing excellent interviews in Nyanza-Lac and Bujumbura. In Bujumbura city, I added a few men who had experience working with urban youth – Adrien, the co-founder, about a decade earlier, of a major urban youth organization that had brought gang members together and played a significant role in calming violence; and Lionel, who had worked for years with the most respected youth organization in Burundi, the Centre Jeunes Kamenge.

Sampling
The categories We wanted to interview a cross-section of people who had been refugees, internally displaced, and those who stayed at home during the war. This proved to be a much more elusive task than expected, as it is very hard to put people into categories that make real-life sense. The category of refugee should be clear: everyone who has not crossed the border is by definition not one. But things are more complicated. Take Pierre, a Tutsi and a driver now. Every time things became too hot in Bujumbura, he went on a boat on Lake Tanganyika and stayed there, moving around until things were calmer. One time, he stayed away for a year, traveling as far as Zambia. He never

set foot in a refugee camp, never got a return package. Do we consider him a refugee or not?

Things are as hard with internally displaced people (IDPs). Easiest to recognize as IDPs are those people who currently still live in displacement camps, typically close to the communal centers. But many Burundians – mainly Hutu – did not flee to these formal sites, but rather fled *away* from the town centers, from the police. They are called 'dispersed' instead of displaced. This was hardly a permanent condition: after a few days or weeks of sleeping in the forest, they would return home, and flee again at another dangerous moment. So, is someone who lives for nine years in a camp in the same category as someone who on six different occasions fled into the forest for a week? Or is it a different category? How many absences from home make you a displaced person? According to the most recent statistics, 52 percent of all Burundians have fled their homes at least once during the war (MINIPLAN 2006: 31).

And many people fall equally into more than one category. Take the story of Innocent, a thirty-three-year-old farmer and boutique owner:

When the war started I had to flee to a camp for displaced people. There, too, things became very hot, and in 1995 I had to flee to Tanzania. In the refugee camp I lived in awful conditions and had lost all hope. I managed to arrange that I was transferred to a camp for 1972 refugees who had a right to plots of land. I, too, eventually managed to get one. I cultivated it and sold my production. I also did some artisanal jobs and sold the products and began acquiring a small capital to do a commerce of dried fish. When returning two years ago, my money was stolen but I did not abandon the *métier*. I still had my bike and I borrowed a bit of money and started a little trade of bread and peanuts. This allowed me to live well in the displacement camp with my wife (who had stayed there when I fled to Tanzania: we had not seen each other for seven years and did not know if the other was still alive, and I was so pleased when I found her again and she had waited for me). When the fields started producing well, I sold part of the land to increase my capital, so now I own a boutique and I pay others to help my wife cultivate the lands. I now live in my own house.

Innocent started as an IDP, became a refugee, then got himself into another refugee camp, then returned to a displacement camp again, and then moved into his own home. What category do we put him in?[1] Note also the stunning dynamism displayed by this man. This is what survival is all about.

In short, the easy categorization we had in mind proved to be very hard to apply to people's lives with any degree of realism. It may do the job adequately when it comes to writing project documents or producing aggregate statistics, but it totally fails to capture the reality of people's lives. Under conditions of protracted war, if one takes a dynamic, rather than a snapshot, view of things, almost nobody's real life falls within a single category (and the usual statistics we see are meaningless). If we were to focus on the more socially relevant level of households, rather than individuals (as we had so far), this would become even more the case.

The places I chose the rural towns we worked in because they had high concentrations of the different categories of people we wanted to interview. Hence, we worked in Ruhororo because it has the country's largest IDP camp; Nyanza-Lac, because it has the highest number of returned refugees; and Busiga because it was one of the calmest communes during the war, and consequently most households stayed home throughout. Within each of these locations, we chose two to three *collines* (literally: hills, the lowest geographic marker for Burundians, consisting of about 150–300 households) and randomly walked through them, day after day, for two weeks or so. We spent about six to seven weeks in each commune.

In each province, we asked the governor and then the communal administrator for permission to work. Most of these people

TOTAL: 388 interviews, sampled by

Age and gender

- 272 men, 116 women
- 245 young (below 30 years old) and 143 adult

Relevant categories

- 82 IDPs, 45 repatriated refugees, 89 stay at home households
- 217 rural people and 171 urban dwellers (incl. 61 migrants)
- Over-sampling on former combatants: 63 child soldiers and adult ex-soldiers, incl. 17 deserters
- Four economic categories: indigent (80), very poor (143), poor (86) and rich (22)

TABLE 2.1 Rural sample by category

	Busiga	Ruhororo	Nyanza-Lac	Total rural
Ex-combatants	6	10[2]	12	28
Repatriated refugees	3	1	35	39
Displaced people	0	37	16	53
People who stayed home	20	30[3]	2	52
Economic migrants	0	0	6	6
Unknown	37[1]	0	3	40
TOTAL	66	78	74	218

Notes: 1. The reason we end up with this large number of 'unknowns' is that we started by doing many focus groups in Busiga: under these circumstances, we could not ask everyone their personal trajectory. But there is no doubt that these are overwhelmingly people who stayed at home. 2. Most of these ex-combatants lived in the IDP camp as well. 3. Overwhelmingly these are people from Banda *colline*.

TABLE 2.2 Urban sample by category

	Kamenge	Musaga	Bwiza	Other urban	Total urban
Ex-combatants	20	9	3	3	35
Repatriated refugees	3	1	1	1	6
Displaced people	16	8	4	1	29
People who stayed home	6	9	8	15	38
Economic migrants	8	33	8	9	58
Unknown	2	2	0	1	5
TOTAL	55	62	24	30	171

were very open toward us: they gave us suggestions, introduced us to people, and generally cared about our subject. Once in the *colline* (or the urban neighborhood), we first met the *chef de colline* to explain what we were doing; often interviewing that person right away as well. Thereafter, we essentially followed a random sampling strategy. We simply walked along minor roads and mere paths and met people who were walking, in front of their house, at the local health center, in the field, etc. Usually, the first day, we were continuously encircled by tens of people, making private interviews pretty hard. By the next day, these numbers would already have decreased – only the kids still running after us. By day three or four, we had become part of the decor: the novelty had worn off. Each day, we would comb a different section of the *colline*, eventually covering most of it.

The urban communes of Kamenge and Musaga were chosen because they reflect the realities of life for the large majority of ordinary urban people. One is almost totally Hutu and the other Tutsi. We also conducted some interviews in Bwiza, a slightly better-off, mixed neighborhood in the center of the city; and with a number of well-off people spread throughout the city – so we had a decent sample of urban people who were non-poor as well.

Age and gender As this research was particularly interested in youth and masculinity, our aim was to talk to two-thirds men, and, within each category, two-thirds young people (below thirty). Contrary to our initial expectation, it was as easy to talk to women as to men. Even in mixed small groups, women talked easily and with confidence. Young women were probably the hardest to reach, although if one could get them alone, they spoke with great ease as well. We ended up very close to our aims. In general, almost half of our sample was composed of young men, although this was more the case in the city than in the countryside. About one quarter was composed of adult men (but as many as twenty-four of those were exactly thirty years old!), and a bit more than one quarter of women, mainly young women.

In Burundi, a stunning 73 percent of the population is below thirty years of age; 46 percent is below fifteen (MINIPLAN 2006: Table 2.7c). Our research focused principally on the fifteen-to-twenty-nine-year-olds – 27 percent of society – the new generation, who grew up during the war, committed most of the violence and suffered most from it, and who will be the builders of the future of their country.

Youths spoke to us with great ease as well, and their analysis was often extremely sophisticated and nuanced. We reached our

TABLE 2.3 Sample by age

	Young men (15–29)	Adult men (≥30)	Young women (15–29)	Adult women (≥30)	Total
Busiga	18	14	19	9	60
Ruhororo	34	20	12	11	77
Nyanza-Lac	27	30	9	5	71
Bujumbura	88	40	34	7	169
Total %	47	26	19	8	
Total %, rural	38	30	19	11	
Total %, urban	52	24	20	4	

goal, as two-thirds of our interviewees were below thirty years old, their average age being twenty-two. The average age of the adults interviewed was forty. The average education level of the entire group was sixth grade. Half of all our interviewees were unmarried – a sure sign of being a 'youth' in Burundian culture, where marriage is the hallmark of adulthood.

We used a simple tool to rank people's households in income categories. In rural areas, it was based on information about the type and number of animals they owned, whether they had off-farm employment,[2] whether they hired people to work for them, and the quality of the house (roof, walls, furniture). In urban areas, we used the last two criteria again and also included the nature of their work (salaried, informal but constant, informal and occasional) as well as their regular mode of transportation (from foot to car). This allowed us to rank people in four categories, from indigent to well off (only 2 percent in the countryside but 20 percent in the city in our sample).

We constantly monitored the interviewee profiles we had obtained and tried to correct if we were far removed from our ideal proportions. The most frequent, hard-to-address imbalance was economic: it was difficult to interview the lowest economic category of (destitute or indigent) people. This difficulty of talking to the poorest is not a surprise. Their houses are not on the road or the path, and they do not stand in the front circle of those who come to greet you. Sometimes the differences were stunning. In the Ruhororo camp, for example, all it required was to move away from the first row of houses along the road: by the third row, one was in a different world, where the houses were all, without exception, shacks with grass roofs, and everyone dressed in rags. People were much more unwilling to talk to us: they hardly looked at us, their long-standing marginality making them feel unworthy of attention, doubt they had anything to say; the low quality of their houses making them feel ashamed to invite an outsider in. In those places, it could take us as much as half an hour to get a person to talk to us. We have interviews there where the person we spoke to never looked us in the eyes, or sat with his back to us – so many signs of internalized inferiority. We did try to do as many of these interviews as possible, but it was a challenge to maintain the energy.

We had early on decided to over-sample two categories: child soldiers and adult ex-combatants. As this research was very interested in understanding conflict dynamics, interviewing this population of overwhelmingly young men was important, and so we interviewed a total of sixty-three of them.[3]

Finally, within all three of the rural locales, we chose to work in at least two *collines*: one in the center of town, easily accessible by road, typically close to the communal offices; and one remote, hard to reach. We did this because we were interested in following up on Marc Sommers' (and, of course, before him, Robert Chambers') argument that 'It always rains in the same place' (2005), i.e. that life in the centers of communes is a lot better than in the peripheries, for it is there that all the infrastructures and programs are concentrated.

Our study confirmed that geographical maldistribution within communes is prevalent. In Busiga, for example, one zone out of three contains the communal offices, three elementary schools, the oldest *lycée*, a health center, and all of this along a moderately good road that itself is the only decent way in or out of town. In Ruhororo, schools, health centers, and the only two functioning secondary schools in the commune were all in the same zone as well. In Nyanza-Lac the situation was less dramatic. There were secondary schools, as well as health centers and primary schools, in all five zones of the commune.

Interestingly, in both Busiga and Ruhororo, the *collines* where the future felt palpably better were the *remote* ones. While there were frequent complaints about missing infrastructures, the economic prospects were better and the sense of future more vibrant in these remote *collines*. The most dramatic case of this is of course the IDP camp of Ruhororo, located close to the commune headquarters, in possession of a health center and a school, and lying on one of the country's major roads. Yet some of the unhappiest people we met, with the most blocked sense of future, were found there. Similarly, in Busiga, people in the remote *colline* of Kimagara seemed more positive in their outlook on life than those in the other *collines*. In Nyanza-Lac, the remote *colline* of Buheka was full of people who looked forward to the future, whereas in Kabongo – a former port, close to the center and connected by a good road – the feelings were much gloomier, with many people complaining about the future, and a lot of angry young men. I have no explanation as to why this is so: I think the reasons are idiosyncratic, but they do suggest that the relation between infrastructure neglect and political conflict or grievance is not as straightforward as Sommers suggests.

Location

As stated, Busiga, in the province of Ngozi, was chosen because the war did not hit it hard. In 1993, there were almost no local pogroms there. Busiga is also less poor than the average for the province: according to CARE data, after the provincial capital town, it has the second-lowest proportion of 'vulnerable households.' Coffee is very productive there, and its population has a reputation of being independent, engaged in trading and smuggling with neighboring Rwanda. Still, it is a poor place. On average, most of the year, most of its inhabitants eat at most two meals a day, of which neither is balanced and only one contains sufficient calories: five months a year, they are below even that low level (Louvain-Développement 2004). The communal administrator told us that population density is 615 persons per square kilometer – a very high number. The economy is almost entirely dependent on agriculture, principally food crops and coffee and bananas as a cash crop.

Ruhororo is located in the same province, maybe 10 miles away from Busiga. It has known much more division and violence. Hundreds of Tutsi died there in pogroms immediately after the 1993 *coup d'état*, and thousands fled to displacement camps. Ruhororo has the dubious distinction of having had, for most of the war period, the largest camp of internally displaced people in all of Burundi, more than twenty thousand people. Ruhororo was also on the path the CNDD/FDD rebels took from their rear bases in Tanzania to their headquarters in the forest of Kibira. Over the years, there were numerous violent confrontations involving rebels, IDP populations, and the army.

We worked in Ruhororo mainly because of its large displacement camp. We spent weeks among the thousands of Tutsi, many of whom have been living for thirteen years in this camp. We also conducted research in a remote *colline* of Ruhororo, Banda, which Tutsi had fled. This allowed for comparison with both the people living in the camp and the people living in Busiga. Pretty much all the people we interviewed in the camp were Tutsi, and almost all those in the *colline* Hutu.

Ruhororo is poorer than Busiga. The proportion of vulnerable households at 32 percent is almost double that of Busiga (18 percent).[4] About four months a year, people declare they have only one meal or less (both unbalanced and insufficient) a day to eat. Their summer months are as good as Busiga's, but they suffer more the rest of the year. This statistic is unfortunately visible in the large number of pot-bellied children we saw, the skin-and-bones adults we talked to. As the commune has no markets on its own territory, its budget is the country's lowest.

Politically, these two communes are bastions of the ruling CNDD/FDD: both mayors are from that party, as is the governor of the province. President Nkurunziza comes from this area. The two communal administrators – a woman in Busiga – were very helpful and gave us carte blanche during our research; we had good conversations with them on a number of occasions. Note that the Tutsi in the IDP camp overwhelmingly voted for UPRONA, the main Tutsi party: they sent three UPRONA representatives to Ruhororo's *conseil communal*.

Our third rural commune, Nyanza-Lac, is on the other side of the country, in the bottom southern corner, tucked against Lake Tanganyika and Tanzania. It contains a good-sized urban center (we did not work there) and a very large rural hinterland. This is also by far the biggest of all communes we worked in, its surface and population easily double those of the others.

We chose Nyanza-Lac because it is the foremost refugee return commune in Burundi. In one of the *collines*, as many as three-quarters of the population consisted of this category, and many of them had spent about a decade abroad – and sometimes, if they were refugees from 1972, more than three decades. In Nyanza-Lac, we primarily interviewed repatriated refugees, but we also spoke to a number of returned IDPs. The region has known many IDP camps as well, but, unlike in Ruhororo, these camps were bi-ethnic and they had entirely emptied out in the last two years.

Nyanza-Lac is a place of contradictions and extremes. Historically, this is one of the richest communes in the country. This whole region has ample income-generating opportunities: palm oil, rice, fishing, manioc, trade over the lake and the road. Food intake is significantly higher in this region: whereas in the north almost one half of the population has a daily caloric intake of 1,400kcal, in the south less than one fifth of the population lives in a household with such a low caloric intake (World Bank 2006: 43).

Notwithstanding its wealth, schooling was neglected in Nyanza-Lac. The commune did not have a single secondary school until 1994. There are two reasons for that. One is clearly a policy of the state not to build schools in many of the country's peripheral areas. The other is the fact that people in Nyanza-Lac were doing economically well and did not feel a major need for education.

The commune's population has been growing fast since the 1970s. A few decades ago, only the coastal strip was inhabited; the rural hinterland was much emptier, covered with dense forest and grazing lands. All this changed after 1972. The violence started in this part of the country and the repression was ferocious: many were killed, many fled, and the commune emptied out. In the subsequent decades, major in-migration took place, both spontaneous and organized by the state: truckloads of people were brought in from other parts of Burundi. These were often people from the poorest and most densely settled regions up north (Gitega, Kayanza) but also from neighboring communes.

Some bought their land, some received it. The communal administrator told us that of the current population of Nyanza-Lac, less than 10 percent has roots there from before 1972.

Politically, this town is Hutu dominated, but closer to opposition parties such as FRODEBU and CNDD-Nyangoma. The mayor belongs to the FRODEBU; he is a repatriated refugee from Tanzania, an extremely friendly and dynamic man, whom we interviewed at length one evening, together with his Tutsi ex-FAB police chief. In this commune, we interviewed many people who were followers of the CNDD-Nyangoma, whose leader is from neighboring Bururi.

Bujumbura city, finally, was chosen – well, because it is Bujumbura: the only major city in the country, source of dreams and fears for all Burundians, and a totally different place from the countryside, whether economically, socially, or politically. We worked mainly in Kamenge and Musaga, two poor neighborhoods at the periphery of the city, almost totally Hutu and Tutsi respectively.

Kamenge was the heartland of the urban violence throughout the civil war. Once multi-ethnic, like the rest of the city, it was the theater of mass violence and became entirely Hutu. Thousands of people were killed in 1994 by the infamous gangs and the army here (Reyntjens 1995: 18). An enormous number of FNL and CNDD/FDD rebels were recruited here (this is reflected in the interviews, for we have many ex-combatants from here). The neighborhood has almost no public services: a few water points, some congested roads, old open sewers. It is located near some major roads, though, providing opportunities for many small traders as well as artisans and informer sector laborers (Observatoire Urbain 2006: 22). This is the poorest urban commune we worked in, with the lowest rate of education (less than 2 percent has tertiary education). Some sectors of the commune are slightly better off: civil servants build houses there, although they typically prefer not to live there. In other sectors, farmers from *Bujumbura rurale* have sought refuge from the continued war with the FNL. The town mayor is FRODEBU, a party that had positioned itself during the elections as more radically pro-Hutu than the CNDD/FDD. He too was extremely friendly and open, very busy dealing with a non-stop stream of people needing help.

Musaga is the Tutsi equivalent of Kamenge, but economically more mixed. As with other places where Tutsi congregated during the war, Musaga is located around a big military camp; the city prison is on its territory as well. It contains a neighborhood that is high middle class; indeed, even some UN foreigners live there. But the rest of Musaga is pretty much as poor as Kamenge. There are only ten public water points for tens of thousands of people, one health center, three primary and two secondary schools, and few other decent infrastructures (Nduwumwami 2006). Politically, the commune is firmly in the Tutsi opposition camp. It is governed by a mayor from PARENA, the party of former president Bagaza, generally seen as very pro-Tutsi.

Bwiza is adjacent to the city center, and has better water and sanitation, more electricity, better roads. Economically it is a step up, with many *petits fonctionnaires* living there, although it is still a far cry from the top neighborhoods where the '*chefs*' and the *bazungu* ('whites') live. Ethnically it has always been mixed, and remained so during the war (although it was not easy for Hutu to live there). It also has a sizeable population of Congolese and other Africans. It remained quite calm during the war: middle-class families of both ethnicities fled there, if they could afford it, to seek refuge from the violence in the rest of the city. It is also a commune with a great many bars.

Finally, I decided to get a better idea of the visions and analyses of some better-educated and wealthier people in the capital. Thus I sent my translators out for a week of interviewing their friends and neighbors and former classmates. This yielded twenty-five or so interviews with people who belonged to economic class 4 – the highest class in my interviews. These people lived in many different neighborhoods. They were typically university-level-educated, older – mid-thirties to fifties – and full-time salaried in the private sector, the international aid community, or the higher levels of the state.

PART TWO

The view from below

3 | Peace and war as read in Burundi[1]

Toward the end of all our interviews, we asked people 'what does peace (*amahoro*) mean to you?' This line of questioning was designed to allow us to take a position in some more theoretical debates. First, I wanted to get an empirical sense of the 'positive peace' versus 'negative peace' debate. This discussion started in the late 1960s, against the backdrop of the cold war (the Vietnam War was waging then) and growing awareness of Third World poverty. Traditional peace research was under attack by a new generation of radical scholars. One of their prime complaints was that researchers focused solely on negative peace, i.e. the absence of war, uncritically elevating this to an absolute ideal. But, critics argued, peace is not simply when people or nations don't fight each other, but when there is cooperation, trust, and respect between them. They were also concerned with social justice: in situations of high exploitation and inequality, is the absence of overt war truly the best possible outcome? Do people really think that there is peace in their lives when they are dis- criminated against? The term positive peace, then, opened the doors to include concerns with justice and social relations. This debate never made much headway in regular security circles,[2] although the current usage of the term 'human security' draws on this intellectual legacy.

Second, I thought it would be of interest to compare people's answers to these questions with the international post-conflict agenda. This agenda contains four main parts, which one finds back, both ideologically and organizationally, in all post-conflict situations. In order of importance, they are security (security sec- tor reform, SSR, demobilization, disarmament and reintegration, DDR), governance (the creation of a democratic polity), develop- ment (economic growth), and justice/reconciliation (Hamre and

Sullivan 2002). These four domains also dominate Burundi's current policy framework, whether in the government's PRSP (Poverty Reduction Strategy Paper) or the UN's Development Assistance Framework (PBC 2006: 5–7).

There is an intuitive logic to this set-up, but it has also been criticized by scholars. Some argue that it is an external agenda, an export of Western neoliberal thinking in both the economic and political realm, but not something people locally desire or are ready for (Gordon 1997; Paris 2002). Others say it is ridiculously unrealistic (Paris 2004; Ottaway 2002; Burnel 2006) and a much-reduced agenda is thus required (Uvin 2007a). This chapter gives an idea of how ordinary Burundians weigh in on these debates.

What does peace mean to Burundians? The overall data

First it must be said that more than half of all Burundians with whom I spoke about this issue employed multi-criteria definitions of peace: they told me that peace was a combination of different goods, which they could not or did not want to separate. Table 3.1 simply presents all definitions by location.

Safety The most frequent definition of peace is clearly one of traditional 'negative peace,' coming in at double the frequency of the next answer. This is clearly the most common meaning of the term *amahoro*, which from a linguistic perspective refers to the opposite of violence: it is about tranquility, calm; as in other languages, it is also used as a greeting – 'peace be with you.'

Most people, when using this definition, talked about the absence of gunshots, of fear. About half of them employed the very same image: 'to sleep at night without fear.' This came back over and over, in rural and urban areas. This answer was over-represented among young men below twenty-two years of age – possibly because they feel at the greatest risk of being killed or enlisted.

A few people offered very strong 'negative peace' definitions, making clear that they intended to limit peace to only that notion, and explicitly excluding any other aspects:

TABLE 3.1 Definitions of peace

| | Rural | | | | Urban | | | |
	Busiga	Ruhororo camp	Ruhororo Colline	Nyanza-Lac	Musaga	Kamenge	Bwiza	Other urban	Total
Safety	19	18	4	14	25	17	9	11	117
Basic needs	7	15	3	8	19	6	3	7	68
Good relations	11	9	2	6	13	12	3	4	60
Mobility	8	4	1	9	8	7	2	3	42
Good governance	2	0	0	7	6	3	0	4	22
Individual	1	2	2	1	0	0	1	2	9
TOTAL	48	48	12	45	71	45	18	31	318

Peace is about eating and sleeping, being able to enjoy the fruits of your work. When there is peace, you can work with a calm spirit. Even if the situation isn't good today, you can have hope for tomorrow as long as you can invest in an activity. (Twenty-eight-year-old male farmer and mason, Nyanza-Lac)

Peace is not hearing gun shots anymore. It is not fleeing one's house. Even if I have to sleep on an empty stomach, I know I will wake up in security. (Twenty-three-year-old unemployed woman, sexual abuse victim, Musaga)

Negative peace answers often included references to theft and criminality.[3] This was principally the case in Busiga, the commune least touched by the war, but which must have had until recently a checkered security record in terms of thefts and banditry. It was also the case in the capital, and especially in the poorest neighborhoods. In other words, in the 'peace equals security' definition, more is included than the absence of war: people also value the absence of crime very much, and they consider there is no peace without it. It is a definition of safety, not 'no war' as such (see too CENAP and NSI 2006).

This close link between peace and criminality reflects the fact that many people have suffered more during the war years from criminality than from direct politically motivated warfare as such. Indeed, the issue that surfaces constantly when people discuss the war years is pillage: it was hard in our conversations to find any family, any person, who was not deeply marked by the theft of their animals, their money, their roofs, their bike, their clothes. For many, this happened repeatedly, including when the peace agreements had been signed already and when the demobilization was already well advanced. In other words, the prime face war took for people was criminality and banditry, and much of this was not necessarily the same as 'THE WAR' in capital letters – the big conflict between clearly defined politico-ethnic parties. If criminality continues or even worsens after the official end of the war, there is not only no peace dividend, but also no peace, period.

One final remark. My sense from the conversations is not so much that criminality and banditry *rise* after war ends (as is usually argued, e.g. Call 2007; Mac Ginty 2006; but doubted by Peters et al. 2003: 28), but rather that they abate too little, or maybe not at all. Criminality and banditry were omnipresent during the war, but they were hidden under cover of the war. When soldiers or rebels pillaged civilians, it may have been to intimidate enemy populations, to nourish themselves, or simply because the opportunity was too juicy to pass up. It is hard for people to know the difference, and the pain is the same. When war ends, this cover is removed, laying bare the criminality underneath it. At the end of the formal war, the same people, with the same guns, the same needs, and the same lack of jobs, are still around – hence the importance of successful demobilization, disarmament and reintegration (DDR) programs.[4]

Basic needs The second-most frequent definition of peace involved basic needs and poverty. Many people told us that there exists no peace without a minimum of material well-being. As a thirty-five-year-old woman in Ruhororo told us: 'How can you have peace if your stomach is empty?' Indeed, the image that dominates this category is overwhelmingly the empty stomach: no peace can exist on an empty stomach. It is not only women telling us that. Here is a quote from a twenty-nine-year-old male migrant peanut seller in Musaga: 'Peace is foremost having bread. If my children and those of my neighbors don't cry of hunger at night I have peace in my heart.'

Different assumptions seem to underlie this statement. First, people are clearly telling us that, for them, peace means nothing without improvements in the quality of life. This confirms scholarship: as Tony Addison (2003: 1) states so well: 'The end of war saves *lives* – including those of the poor who are often its main victims – but it may not deliver much if any improvement in *livelihoods*.' This is confirmed by the fact that this definition seems to occur most frequently in places where there has been major suffering from the war and where there is significant social discontent that nothing has changed since the end of the war (Ruhororo; Kamenge). Second, a minority of people seem to adhere to a version of the core belief held by development professionals everywhere, namely that civil wars occur because of poverty. As a young man we met herding cows in a remote *colline* of Busiga told us:

> There are different levels to peace. One is individual – that you are not sick and hungry. Another is mutual understanding, that there is no discrimination. My own life is at peace, but that is not the case for all of us: the individual dimension is often lacking. People are often hungry and sick, they have heavy debts and family conflicts, and that can disrupt peace.

Or this twenty-five-year-old male migrant to Musaga, with no education: 'Peace is when nobody is a victim of injustice. It is also when the entire neighborhood has enough to eat. If your neighbor doesn't have what is needed you too become vulnerable.' Or this twenty-nine-year-old mechanic in a better-off urban neighborhood: 'People must have work and quit poverty: if they don't, they start thinking badly of each other, because they feel bad themselves.' For this minority, there is a causal link between poverty and peace.

Social peace The third-most frequent answer defined peace as 'good social relations.' This definition, too, is more holistic than simply about the absence of war. It privileges social relations, cohabitation, social harmony.

> If we live in the same place and understand each other there will be peace. (Twenty-one-year-old woman, Busiga)

> Peace is when people live together and share, they don't kill each other but help each other. There is almost peace now, so there is hope. (Thirty-year-old male student from the interior, living in 'Chechnya,' a very poor neighborhood in Musaga)

There are no particular regional variations in this answer. It

48

comes back everywhere as a major undercurrent, either as part of broader definitions or as a single criterion. Note that, running counter to crude gender expectations of women as nurturing and focused on relations, women do *not* employ the food definition or the social relations definition more frequently than men do.

Mobility A surprisingly large number of answers related peace to mobility. For example:

> Peace is being free to move around and visit friends and family. (Twenty-four-year-old female, remote *colline* in Busiga)

> When you can visit others there is peace. (Eighteen-year-old man, Ruhororo IDP camp)

> A place where you can come and go as you wish, that is peace. (Twenty-year-old male student, Bwiza)

Even though Burundians are not very mobile – in many provinces, more than 80 percent of people have not visited anyone during the last year (MINIPLAN 2006: 32) – they do consider the possibility of doing so very important. I believe that the surprising importance of mobility in defining peace in Burundi relates to three factors. First, it refers back to times more innocent, before the war began. A few times in Ruhororo, for example, we heard the same image that peace means 'you can go for a long walk and sleep where you arrive: you can knock on the door, you can sleep there and you will continue your voyage the next morning.' This image is powerful in people's minds. All older people I asked tell me that when they were young, this really was how things happened in Burundi until the 1980s.[5] From this perspective, the mobility definition is about the restoration of the former social capital order, a sign of the desire for continuity amid dramatic change.

Second, during the war, insecurity and chaos forced people to lead lives that were awfully akin to imprisonment. IDPs and refugees were literally stuck in their respective camps; many Hutu retain very bad memories of the awful *camps de regroupement*,

49

where they were forcibly herded like cattle; and urban dwellers were ethnically cleansed into segregated neighborhoods. From this perspective, the mobility definition is about security and the state.

Finally, I surmise that mobility is generally a symbol of well-being: when people talk about the good life or about dreams for the future, they frequently use images of mobility as well. A better life is one in which one can move around, can go to places – whether the city or abroad – and can avail oneself of opportunities that are available there. Not surprisingly, then, this answer occurred most frequently among young people, especially those between twenty-one and thirty: they are establishing a new life and mobility to them is crucial.

Peace as good governance Few definitions of peace referred to the major political stakes the war was fought about – the composition of government, human rights, etc. When they were mentioned, it was usually in combination with other definitions of peace:

> There is no peace now, for as long as there are political chicaneries in Bujumbura, these problems can spread throughout the country. The situation remains unstable. We have a saying: the light comes from the capital and shines over all the country. (Fifty-six-year-old ex-combatant farmer, Nyanza-Lac)

> Peace for me is when the country is on the right path, meaning that there is respect for the human rights of all, freedom for all, punishment of criminals and all people who do wrong in respect of the law. (Thirty-four-year-old seller of charcoal, Musaga)

Clearly, Burundians do not spontaneously define peace in national political or governance terms. This is probably because they feel far removed from national politics, and our conversations focused on their own lives. Most of the minority who constitute the exception to this rule consist of people who are politically angry. These answers occur almost never in the two communes in Ngozi province we visited, nor in Kamenge – all strongholds of the CNDD/FDD. They are much more frequent, however, in Musaga (dominated by a strong Tutsi party) and Nyanza-Lac (a town where we found frequent opposition feelings toward the current government). For many of those who used a 'peace as governance' definition, this was an indirect way of critically commenting on the current government.

Conclusion We should not force all definitions of peace into a single category, as if there is one integrated definition, spoken by one composite Burundian. The people I spoke to used different definitions, in part because they had different opinions at the time I spoke with them – they were different individuals, after all, with different life stories and values; also, the flow of each conversation was different. Still, taken together, these different dimensions are revealing of what peace means to Burundian society.

Half of all people gave us multiple-criterion definitions. This is in line with a recent move in international discourse toward human security, which is precisely based on the notion that freedom from fear cannot be separated from freedom from want. More generally, there clearly seems to exist a widespread sense among Burundians that peace can be understood only in a broad, integrated, 'positive peace' manner.

It seems to me that the way Burundian society defines peace is well represented in the post-conflict agenda – thus contradicting the academically popular but simplistic notion that this is all a mere neocolonial agenda. The first three categories – accounting for 80 percent of all answers – are the exact categories that the international community privileges: security, development, and the restoration of social relations. This is good news: even though peace-building experts and ordinary Burundians use different terms, they seem to talk about the same things. Evidently, when it comes to actual practice, this congruence may start falling apart. In my conversations, for example, there was significant interest among people in opportunities for dialogues and interactions. They talked with pleasure about football matches, concerts, dialogues, radio programs, etc. At the same time, what preoccupies

the international community is transitional justice – a truth commission and a judicial mechanism – which people rarely spontaneously talked about in our seven months. So, it is one thing
to be on the same wavelength regarding the overall direction,
and quite another to implement this in concrete actions.

The most surprising absence was the governance dimension.
When Burundians think of peace, they very rarely explicitly mention governance. This seems to constitute a difference from the
approach by the international community, which is rather ob-
sessed with governance in post-conflict situations, whether it is
the rapid and strong push toward full democracy, or the constant
human rights scrutiny many post-conflict regimes are subjected
to. Burundian society's attitude seems to support Roland Paris's
notion of holding off on democracy while institutionalizing
the state first: national politics or elections are not the key to
Burundians' sense of progress in life immediately at the end of the
war, but safety and economic progress and social relations are.

This may be an incomplete understanding. Most of the key
variables Burundians discussed in their vision of peace 'objectively' have major governance components. Security, for example,
is obviously a core governance matter. The fact that the war ended
is due to the Arusha negotiations and their implementation. And
research also shows that the feeling of security Burundians have
stems not only from the absence of overt war but also from the
knowledge that their army and police forces are now bi-ethnic
up to the highest levels (CENAP and NSI 2006). Finally, let's face
it, there will not be much development without rule of law and
a fight against corruption – also governance matters. Hence, it
seems we can conclude for now that governance is objectively
important, but subjectively not high on Burundians' immediate
post-conflict agenda. But at the same time there are selected
governance issues that have wide popular grounding – as this and
the following chapters show, in Burundi security-sector reform
is clearly one of them, as is the fight against corruption and the
provision of basic services.

There are not many other researchers who have asked people

in post-conflict countries what peace means to them. But for those who did, the answers are generally very similar. Donini and his colleagues (2005), for example, conclude a similar study in Afghanistan, Kosovo, and Sierra Leone as follows:

> [L]ocal communities view security as safety from physical harm and abuse but also extending far beyond to encompass a sense of well-being including elements such as employment, access to basic services, political participation, and cultural identity. ... Thus communities have a more holistic understanding of what constitutes security than the narrower concerns of the two other sets of actors [international development and security ones; Miyazawa 2005 obtained the same results in post-conflict Bougainvillea].

Donini and his colleagues add interesting information I did not explicitly collect: they asked the same question of people working for peace-support organizations (PSOs) and for aid agencies (AAs) and were thus able to compare these definitions of security with those of ordinary citizens. Their conclusion:

> perceptions of security differ significantly among the three sets of actors. Within the context of their mission objectives, the military contingents that characterized PSOs understand security first and foremost in terms of 'force protection,' that is, the need for protection of their own personnel from attacks and threats of attack. PSO perceptions of the security needs of AAs and local communities are viewed through those lenses. While AAs are also concerned about insecurity as it impinges on their ability to carry out their assistance and protection activities, they are more likely to take risks in the interests of carrying out their tasks. They also tend to have a better understanding of how socio-economic issues impact on security and generally have a better grasp than PSOs do of the concerns of local populations.

I believe that these results hold for Burundi as well. 'Security' for the UN is primarily, far and away, its own security.[6] When I did this research, the security requirements of the UN and much of the international community could only be called ridiculous. They were far beyond anything resembling a realistic assessment of danger, and on a totally different planet from what Burundians themselves have to live through each day, including during the height of the war. UN employees were still traveling through the country only with armed escorts: cars with armed soldiers followed their own large, gleaming-white four-wheel-drive vehicles everywhere, and constant satellite communication with HQ at all times was the norm. Of course, the security concerns – and associated benefits in terms of hazard pay – are not the only factors that create these social differences: the enormous social and economic differences have the same effect.[7] Most UN people never leave the capital: instead one can find them behind the high walls, with control towers, barbed wire, and guards everywhere, which the locals call 'Guantánamo.' At night, they congregate together, in the same neighborhoods and bars, where the only locals are the absolute top elite of the country and a few NGO upstarts who are comfortable around the internationals. This all holds for most of the international community.

This is more than a waste of money. It squanders scarce social capital, contributing to the notion that there is a radical difference between the internationals and the locals. In post-conflict situations, then, the international community has the widest mandate, the strongest principles and ideas, and the most power (for governments are weak and profoundly aid-dependent). Yet, at the same time, these are also the countries where the people representing the international community are most ignorant of what is truly happening outside their offices, and the most dependent on small groups of intermediaries of sometimes unclear provenance. This situation persists long after the widespread insecurity has abated. This should give pause for thought to all would-be missionaries.

Security now

I also asked people how security was in their neighborhoods, their *collines*. The answers overwhelmingly indicated that current security is good – or at least, much better than in the recent past. Our conversations also show that this is a strong source of legitimacy for the current government and the president.

Each place had its own history of security. In Nyanza-Lac, the answer to the question was very often accompanied by a spontaneous discussion, with anecdotes, on how bad it used to be there, and a heartfelt expression of happiness that things were much better now. In urban neighborhoods, it was regularly accompanied by a qualifier, a hedging, owing to the sense that banditry is still a problem there.

In Bujumbura city, different social classes had their own particularities. In the poor slums of Musaga and Kamenge, a sizeable segment of the population complained about banditry. The tone of most conversations was that it had decreased but it was not over yet. Theft of bikes and of money; drunkenness and the aggression that frequently accompanies it; sexual violence or the risk thereof – these all came up rather frequently in these conversations, with obvious gender differences.

The better off and better educated our interviewees were, however, the more frequently they conveyed a sense of the precariousness of security based on a *political* analysis of the situation:

Security is good but precarious. Everything can explode at any time because of the current political tensions. (Thirty-three-year-old male bank manager, university graduate)

Security is still relative. The minds are not calmed down yet. Our place is still full with rebels and demobilized who could create disorder at any moment. (Forty-four-year-old male manager in the public sector, one year of university)

This may reflect a number of trends. First, these conversations all took place in late 2006, when the political climate was particularly tense, following the incarceration on trumped-up coup charges of opposition politicians and the regular intimidation of journalists. Second, more of the people interviewed in this category were Tutsi, and, while they were not necessarily vehemently opposed

to the government, distance if not distrust was their default attitude. Third, as in the definition of peace, the people giving these
answers were making national-level arguments: this is the level
where their attention is directed, where they see their citizenship
playing out. The implicit reference point of the majority of the
poor we interviewed was local – the *colline* or the neighborhood.
Fourth, this is clearly a more 'intellectual' reasoning, based on
more complicated and long-term political causal relationships.

I did not ask explicit questions about the role of the police
or the army in this overall sense of (in)security. A small number
of people spontaneously attributed the improvement in security
they discussed to the deployment of more police in the commune. On the negative side, among those who complained about
persistent insecurity or ill governance, dissatisfaction with the
police came up at times. This is in part related to an underlying
unease about the ethnic question: many of the new policemen
on the streets are former CNDD-FDD rebels, which creates unease in these predominantly Tutsi streets. The unease may be
twofold – with the evident and blatant ethnic otherness of these
people, and with the sense of risk and danger associated with
all ex-combatants: they still carry guns, and who knows what
goes on in their heads!

A personal anecdote will illustrate this. One night I was going
out with a few young men from Musaga. We were walking the
streets together, at about 9.30 p.m., after a beer in a local bar.
Suddenly my young companion whispered to me, 'Peter, watch
out, there are CNDD rebels there, ahead of us.' I, of course,
in typical *Muzungu* (white person) fashion, saw nothing: it was
dark, and there were people everywhere, and I wouldn't have
recognized one from another if my life depended on it. My friend
pointed to the right, where, under the shadow of a tree, two
policemen stood looking at us, easily 20 meters away still. I asked
my friend, 'How do you know they are rebels?' and he answered,
almost poetically, 'Look at their eyes, Peter, look at their eyes!'
Unsurprisingly, the policemen stopped us, and a lengthy conversation followed, polite, but with a distinct element of menace in

it. Everyone was making themselves as small as possible before these people with their guns, and their bloodshot eyes with the hepatitis yellow, their ragged clothes. They are so skinny and they behave as if they are delirious – hunger, drinks, a combination of the two? When we were finally allowed to go on, my companion asked me, 'Did you see their eyes? These are the eyes of crazy men. They have seen too much. They have caused too much suffering. They are hungry, Peter, they don't have enough to eat. They have no morals.'

4 | 'If I were in charge here': Burundians on respect, corruption, and the state[1]

'I would not accept to be a communal administrator with the current government, because the national resources are not invested for all but are in the pockets of a few people in power only. I cannot be a leader of the famished.' (Forty-six-year-old taxi driver, Bujumbura)

In the previous chapter, we argued that while democratic governance is one of the central pillars of the international post-conflict/ peace-building enterprise, Burundians rarely explicitly included governance in their definition of peace. But this is not the end of the story. Our conversations reveal that matters of governance and citizenship *are* important to ordinary Burundians in many ways.

The most directly relevant question we posed to approach this subject was one of our favorites: 'If you suddenly became *administrateur communal* tomorrow, what is the first thing you would do?' There was usually an amused smile on people's lips when they heard the question, and they almost always had ideas, often very concrete ones. But insights about governance appeared in many other parts of the conversation as well. Corruption came up a great deal, especially when talking about aid and the state.

Citizenship

The hundreds of answers I received to the 'communal administrator' question crystallized in six categories. The first one, not surprisingly, was basic needs – 'I would help the poor like me,' or, more frequently, 'I would create jobs for the people.' The second category consisted of calls for infrastructure – roads and markets in the countryside, water and roads in the city. Both these will be

TABLE 4.1 Respect and the rule of law

	Rural	Urban	Total
Basic needs	55	70	125
Infrastructure	39	33	72
Listen/respect	32	28	60
Rule of law	25	35	60
Conflict resolution	14	17	31
Delinquency	6	17	23

discussed in the chapter on development: they reflect people's desperate need for improvements in their life conditions. Conflict resolution and the fight against delinquency are discussed in the chapters on security and justice respectively. Here, I focus on answers 3 and 4.

The 'listen/respect' category came back everywhere, often in a passionate manner. A few quotes will give an impression of what I put under this heading:

I would be closer to the local people and listen to them more. I would encourage freedom of expression, so that people would talk. I would make sure that the administration would have close relationships with people, so that they would not get lies. (Eighteen-year-old former child soldier, now taxi-*vélo* driver, Busiga)

I would listen to everyone, rich and poor. This is rarely done in Burundi (Nineteen-year-old woman, Busiga)

The first thing I would do is to let the little people express themselves, listen to everyone and apply justice without bias. (Thirty-year-old female farmer, Ruhororo, Banda *colline*)

I'd assure an impartial social justice. I'd give the same consideration to everyone, the big and the small. (Twenty-four-year-old woman, ex-IDP, Musaga)

Young people are strongly represented among those who talk about this, both in rural and urban areas. This suggests that there is a slow generational shift going on in Burundi.

This type of answer is tied with, and closely related to, another type that I called 'rule of law,' which deals with equal justice for all, combating corruption and clientelism, and the like.

> I would fight corruption, so that the rich and poor receive the same equal treatment. (She then gave examples of land appropriation and bribes in courts; thirty-year-old female farmer, Busiga)

> I would help people in conflict without asking for anything first. I'd make sure emergency aid lists are made in an honest way and include all that need it. (Nineteen-year-old girl, Busiga)

> I'd favor social justice with impartiality, and without trying to favor family members or friends. I would not take decisions all alone but consult my advisors. I'd fight corruption and would sanction those who engage in embezzlement. (Nineteen-year-old migrant man, works in a boutique, Musaga)

> If I had the power, I'd do a lot for the small people and I'd fight corruption a lot. (Twenty-one-year-old FNL self-demobilized, no education at all, Kamenge)

The 'rule of law' category is the most equally shared type of answer across income groups in our interviews: from the poorest to the richest income group, a significant group of people care about it, and this tendency is especially pronounced in Bujumbura.

The 120 answers – fully one third – that I grouped under 'listen/respect' and 'rule of law' are clearly the starting points for a discussion of people's opinions about governance in Burundi. The quotes above show Burundians talking about what people in the international community call non-discrimination, rule of law, and citizenship – even if the Burundians themselves don't use those terms. And they do this across all divides – rural or urban, rich or poor, regardless of their trajectory during the war.

This suggests that there is in Burundi a deep current of attachment to notions very similar to those of the good governance and human rights agendas.

These same images of citizenship and equality come back in other questions. One of the more frequent profiles people described to us when we asked them whom they admire is 'someone who listens to others, even if you are unequal,' or 'people who do not oppress others.' This came back in rural and urban areas.

> I admire a person of justice, who can be trusted to keep secrets, who is impartial. Our *chef de colline* is such a person. (Twenty-one-year-old farmer, Busiga)

> I admire every person who listens to the big and the small equally. There are administrators who, when a poor person launches a complaint, don't listen at all. (Thirty-five-year-old female farmer, Ruhororo *colline*)

> I admire someone who discriminates against no one, who acts for the good of others. In the IDP camp there was a *chef* like that. He intervened in a difficult situation to witness and save the life of a neighbor who was unjustly accused. (Nineteen-year-old female, Nyanza-Lac)

> I admire the *chef de quartier* of Mirango. He is just and honest. If he has to make lists of people of a certain category, orphans for example, he doesn't put anyone on the list who doesn't belong to that category, even if people try to corrupt him. (Twenty-nine-year-old female, Kamenge)

Being listened to, being treated with respect and equity, the absence of corruption – these are matters that Burundians feel in daily life. People judge the reality of their interactions with the state with clear criteria, and they find this reality wanting. The reference point they used to make these judgments, I believe, is a combination of values associated with Western-style democracy as well as values deriving from the traditional institution of *bashingantahe*.

The institution of bashingantahe

One of the key institutions in pre-colonial Burundi was the *bashingantahe*. It consisted of men, designated by their community, and selected on the basis of their wisdom, impartiality, knowledge, and wealth (Trouwborst 1962: 148). Their role was to give advice in local conflicts and to propose judgments. The institution was non-ethnic: Hutu or Tutsi could, and did, become *bashingantahe* (singular: *mushingantahe*). It was not hereditary: each person had to earn the position through his behavior, his words, his slow learning. It is said that if even one member of the community disagreed with the investiture of a *mushingantahe*, it could not proceed.

This institution did not survive Burundi's colonial period in its traditional form. Under the colonial administration and later the post-independence regimes, *bashingantahe* were increasingly nominated from above, obliged to apply formal law, and limited in their power. Eventually, by the 1980s, all state and party officials came to be called by this appellation, and the term came to mean little more than 'sir.' Even during my interviews I noticed that my translators at times presented me to people with this term, using it in its generic form of person of wealth and prestige.

At the same time, 'real' *bashingantahe* persist. They are often referred to by the designation '*bashingantahe investi*,' i.e. those who went through the traditional investiture ceremony, as opposed to those who are just self-proclaimed or being accorded mere terms of politeness. It is not clear how many there are today or what their role and legitimacy are. In our conversations, a handful of people identified themselves as being '*bashingantahe investi*,' and a larger number spoke about them, sometimes positively and sometimes negatively. The institution is certainly still alive, but it functions more haphazardly, and in competition with many other systems of resolving conflicts (which also don't function well).

Their role during the war was ambiguous. In some places, such as Busiga and Nyanza-Lac, we were told that the *bashingantahe* gave advice that prevented 'hot-headed young men' from killing and looting, and that they thus maintained the peace; people were proud of that. In other communes, most notably Ruhororo, this was not the case: people told us that the *bashingantahe* themselves were killed, or simply not listened to.

The issue of *bashingantahe* corruption was often mentioned in conversations. Traditionally, after a decision, as the parties' disagreement was settled, beer would be drunk by all those involved, including a special offering of beer to the *mushingantahe*. But now, we were repeatedly told, the *bashingantahe* ask for beer *before* agreeing to get involved, and will make decisions in favor of the one who managed to pay them in beer. Whether this is exactly what takes place is not clear; rather, this story describes a perversion of what beer is about – from a gift of appreciation to a condition, a bribe – and it reflects growing complaints about the functioning of the institution.

Many Burundians and the international community are interested in restoring the institution of *bashingantahe* (Dexter and Ntahombaye 2005). For many people, this institution provides a crucial indigenous basis on which to rebuild Burundi, or to face the post-conflict challenges of transitional justice and land reallocation. The Arusha agreements, among other 'cultural' stipulations, talk about the 'rehabilitation of the institution of *Ubushingantahe*' (Protocol I, article 7, para. 27). In 2005, a National Council of Bashingantahe was created by constitutional fiat; trainings were given to *bashingantahe* in various places, and they were – and still are – included in all plans regarding transitional justice.

The current government, however, is distinctly less enthusiastic about *bashingantahe* (ibid.; Vandeginste 2006). As it seeks primarily to establish its full control over the territory, it is wary of a corps of people with major public roles who are entirely uncontrolled – a parallel network of local power, so to speak. One way to reduce the power of the *bashingantahe* has been the creation of deliberate confusion: the newly elected members of the '*conseil de colline*,' the lowest level of public administration, are now given the title of '*elected bashingantahe*,' with presumably the same prerogatives as the 'invested' ones. This has created significant local conflicts.

While the high politics of the institution of *bashingantahe* is ambiguous, our conversations clearly show that the values that underlie this institution are still deeply alive among Burundians. When asked 'Whom do you admire?' Burundians responded:

Someone who is objective and can solve conflicts peacefully, someone who can give good advice to others. (Twenty-five-year-old farmer and part-time employee of the civil register of the zone, nine years of education, Busiga)

A person who practices justice, tells the truth, and lives peacefully together with his neighbors, who takes care of the well-being of others. (Thirty-two-year-old demobilized ex-FAB, taxi-*vélo* driver, Ruhororo camp)

Someone who in a conflict advises the parties without bias. (Twenty-two-year-old female farmer, Ruhororo *colline*)

Someone who is just and honest, who manages conflicts that are entrusted to him by others well. (Twenty-three-year-old migrant taxi-*vélo* driver, Kamenge)

Or listen to this: late in the research, one of my assistants, Adrien, on his own initiative, decided to start asking a new question to the youth he found in Bujumbura: 'What is a man?' Most of the people he was talking to at that time were self-demobilized ex-combatants – angry young men with years of violence behind them, of low educational level, mostly unemployed. Hear the power of values in these voices – such beauty, after all the pain and anger:

I think my friends expect that I be a man of my word, a true *mushingantahe*, a man who takes care correctly of his family without forgetting his immediate and further away environment. (Eighteen-year-old)

For me, a man is someone who tries to listen and understand

the others, someone who is just, who doesn't discriminate and has no biases. (Twenty-eight-year-old)

To me, being a man is not simply having a woman, or having money. A man is about the *parole*: a word of honor, of truth, of wisdom. (Twenty-one-year-old)

To me, a man is a *parole* of honor, without lies, someone who speaks the truth and wisdom in his family and community, who is just, without biases and favoritism. (Twenty-three-year-old)

In short, throughout many of the conversations, and in response to many different questions, Burundians told us not so much about specific *bashingantahe* as about the values associated with the institution. These values are clearly still deeply alive in Burundi. People admire others who behave in this way; they would like to be treated that way by the authorities and anyone who has power over them; they dream of themselves living up to those standards.

The values embedded in the institution of *bashingantahe*, it seems, are Burundians' equivalent to human rights (similar to An-Na'im 1992). This is an overstatement: these values are not identical to those underlying human rights – they are not universally applicable, for example, and they have some serious limitations regarding gender and procedure that would be hard to accept under human rights law (Donnelly 1989). But socially, they are the foundation for the key principles of human rights – non-discrimination, dignity, equality of treatment, fairness and reliability.

One of the most important differences from the international human rights or good governance value systems is more subtle, though. Transparency never came up in this discussion, nor did separation of powers or justiciability or procedures of accountability or any other of the structural features human rights and democracy specialists usually talk about. For Burundians, the desired features of citizenship are in people's hearts and minds and attitudes – not in structures of openness or counter-power.

If a person has what it takes, one can have faith in that person doing the right thing, making wise decisions. Much of our Western and international ideology of democracy, human rights, and good governance is based on structures, on regulations, on the organization of counter-power and institutional checks and balances. While Burundians were often talking about the same aims, they did so in terms of people: they spontaneously desire 'better people' rather than 'better structures.'

Corruption

Corruption was the most-discussed public item in our conversations.[2] The acknowledged facts about corruption do not contradict what the people told me. Reports published by OLUCOME, a local corruption watchdog, between 1998 and 2006 document more than 159 billion Burundian francs stolen by corrupt officials, and reality is likely to be far ahead of what is published (in 2006, one US dollar equaled about 1,000 Burundian francs). Transparency International ranks Burundi among the world's most corrupt countries.

Burundian intellectuals often say that corruption is a phenomenon born of the war. This is wrong. I spent a lot of time in Burundi in the 1980s, and the recollections I have of that period are of systematic corruption and clientelism, embedded in the very seams of society – part of the constellation of causes of the war rather than a consequence of it. Why is this argument, then, so popular among many Burundian intellectuals? I can see three different reasons. First, back then, the media were all owned by the government: corruption by those in power was not publicly discussed. Second, the people who make this argument grew up in the old system, and are in many ways products of it. To them, things in Burundi started going wrong when the war began; before, Burundi was a nice place. All social ills are thus attributed to the war. Third, corruption did indeed become more visible, more brutal, during the war. There were fewer resources to distribute and the state was weaker. There was a dramatic switch to humanitarian assistance, which can easily be diverted by the many intermediaries who select their own families and friends as beneficiaries, hand out less and sell the rest, and so on. This holds for immediate post-war reconstruction programs as well.

In conversations with ordinary Burundians, most references to corruption occur in the context of international aid – mostly emergency aid, but also development aid. A few examples out of tens will suffice:

> No organizations have helped me. There is humanitarian aid which often doesn't reach our *colline*, but stays near the communal office. This is due to management, not because of distance from the *colline*. (Twenty-year-old married woman, Busiga)

> When the lists of *sinistrés* [disaster victims] are made for humanitarian aid, either the wrong names are on it, or when the distribution comes, people are given too little. The rich stand by and buy the remaining sacks and sell it for a profit in their boutiques. This is done publicly, they don't even hide it. (Fifty-five-year-old very poor female IDP, Ruhororo)

> There were people here who came to support associations. But the way they chose the members was wrong. They took people depending on whether they were friends with the *chef* or not. Recruitment ignored the poor, the small people. [...] We were told to build seven foot by five foot houses and then we would receive roofing, but once we did it, we only got enough roofing for two-thirds of the roof. The rest had been taken by the employees who distribute the roofing. [...] Goats were distributed to friends of the *chef*, but not to the repatriates. [...] To be allowed to work on the building of a new school, we had to pay the foreman first. (Twenty-nine-year-old man, living off different small jobs, Nyanza-Lac)

The reason corruption comes up when ordinary people talk about international aid is not because aid agencies are uniquely corrupt – far from it – but because this is one of the few flows of money or goods that come close to the poor (or are designed to do so), and hence corruption and mismanagement here are very visible and painful.

Some of these accusations of corruption seemed excessive or almost ritualistic. Take, for example, this obviously better-off farmer who, after telling us he did not get emergency aid (targeted at the most vulnerable), immediately added that this was owing to corruption; or this demobilized soldier, who complained that he was refused emergency aid from other agencies (this is standard policy, as the assumption is that the agencies should focus on those people who have received nothing yet) and explained that this was due to corruption. Even in the quotations above, I am not so sure that the last one is factually entirely correct. What does this tell us? For one, the evident fact that we should investigate these matters more thoroughly: neither silence about corruption nor, necessarily, accusations about it are automatically true. But it muddies the water on more than empirical grounds. As Dan Smith (2007: 9), in his excellent study of corruption in Nigeria, suggests:

> Arguably, the idea of corruption has become an organizing lens through which people in many contemporary societies explain and lay blame for a range of failings with regard to democracy, development, and other expectations of modernity. [...] It is [...] quite remarkable how widely the concept of corruption has been adopted and appropriated by people in developing countries as a way of talking about, understanding, and sometimes resisting aspects of inequality and injustice in their societies. As an organizing idea for understanding the world (and as a set of practices) corruption can be both a strategy of the powerful and a weapon of the weak.

Corruption has become a short-cut accusation, a term used by those who are angry at the system to express dissatisfaction and cast aspersions. It is a (rhetorical) weapon of the weak – all the more credible as there indeed *is* a lot of corruption in Burundi. This is related to what we ended the previous section with, where we said that Burundians desire 'better people' rather than 'better structures.' Corruption as described by Burundians is a 'bad person's' fault – not a structural issue. Corruption, then, is in part to the masses what human rights are to the well educated. Both are ways to 'stick it to the man,' terms whose currency in protest and dissatisfaction is useful. Hence, more than simply accurate descriptions of a social fact, talking about these things is a political act – a way the jargon of the international community has become reappropriated in local political struggles. Given that in Burundi both corruption and human rights violations are indeed prevalent, this makes understanding these discourses very complicated.

It takes deep knowledge of Burundian society and trust by Burundians, which few foreigners ever acquire, to get a sense of the real extent and mechanisms of corruption. Almost always, when aid-related corruption in Burundi is uncovered, it is because a Burundian told a foreigner – foreigners cannot figure it out for themselves. What is required for foreigners to effectively combat corruption includes: the trust of local employees to learn what is really going on in terms of hiring and firing people; a detailed knowledge of real prices on local markets; and knowledge of rumors in the street about the reputation and social networks of the relevant agency's personnel. This runs oddly counter to the usual approach to dealing with corruption by almost all agencies, which is to send in a foreigner to control the money. It is not foreign expertise/control which is required, but profound internal workplace changes – clearly much harder to initiate. And hence the charade of the foreign money controller continues, with little impact.

Historical interlude: long-term changes in people's attitudes toward governance and corruption

There are two historical elements that set Burundi apart from most other African countries. First, the weakness of social structures apart from the family. Burundians did – and still do – not live in villages but in isolated homesteads, spread out throughout the country. All early scholars agree that the only center of a

69

Burundian's life was his family. Typically, one's neighbors are one's family, and while there is a sense of joint belonging to a *colline*, that is hard to separate from belonging to an extended family. People do have broader networks of friends and advisors, but these have no formal role. There are no traditional village chiefs or masters of ceremony, no age groups or secret societies. In short, then, Burundian social life has long been very non-hierarchical and atomized, focused around individual nuclear families.

At the same time, Burundi was a kingdom, a centralized state, long before European colonizers arrived, with largely the same borders as the current state. Although the king ruled the country, most local power was held by princely families of Ganwa, assisted by Tutsi *sous-chefs* (with some Hutu among them as well). Burundians have a longer history of 'being Burundian,' of being members of a Burundian state, than many other Africans have of an equivalent status. Much of this system survived until well into independence, bringing Ziegler (1971: 14) to exclaim that 'the Tutsi state represents probably the most complex and the least culturally influenced traditional society that exists today in Africa.'

All descriptions of Burundi's pre-colonial system describe a society in which clientelism and person-driven rule dominated (Trouwborst 1962; Ziegler 1971; Laely 1997). Land and cattle – the two most important items for economic and social survival – were attributed through personal dependencies, clientelistic structures of subordination at different levels – from king to Ganwa to chiefs to *sous-chefs*, etc. Thomas Laely's work is among the most revealing on this:

> The structures of government and administration of the pre-colonial monarchy were not determined by permanently given territorial units; they were dependent on personal relationships of the moment, and were shaped according to the pattern of patron–client dealings. This resulted in what might be described as multi-layered, overlapping pyramids of people being depend-

ent on each other. [...] The fact that so much was arranged on an informal basis resulted in favourites, and even personal clients, greatly influencing the day-to-day work of government and administration. They can be classified as 'anonymous' or 'proto' functionaries since none held any specific, differentiated official position. [...] Bearing in mind that such a subtle hierarchy and pattern of stratification was determined in many ways by multiple intersecting variables, there could be no generalised access to political authorities by universal rules, but only highly personalised and very particularised ways of approach.

And Ziegler (1971: 54) says that 'social structures of Burundi are of constant fluidity.' When the colonizer came, a formal layer was added on top of this proto-state, but it was a weak one. On the one hand, the colonizer formally abolished the personalized positions and clientelist relations of the past, replacing them with the trappings of the modern state: fixed taxes to the state instead of tributes to patrons, written law instead of custom, formal equality of all instead of cattle clientship,[3] bureaucrats instead of allies. On the other hand, the layer of the modern state that was grafted on top applied basically only to the whites and, slowly, to the urban bureaucrats who became part of this system; its extension farther into the country was theoretical rather than real.[4] For ordinary people, nothing much changed in how they were governed, except that local authorities imposed many more demands on them and inequality became stronger.

It is this system that, in 1962, became independent, with little preparation. During the very last years before independence, the Belgians had organized elections, but these had not fundamentally altered the system: those who were elected were overwhelmingly traditional leaders, and the people continued to behave toward them on the basis of traditional allegiance and clientship, rather than democratic citizenship, which most of them had never known (ibid.: 63, 69). As Ziegler describes it in 1971:

Since 1962, Burundi lives in a strange juridical situation. Almost the entirety of the five principal strata of the nation – the King and his family, the Baganwa, the Tutsi, the Hutu and the Twa – remain ferociously attached to the Burundian cosmology, model their behavior on traditional motivations and scrupulously respect the social order as it has been handed down by custom and oral tradition. At the same time, those in charge of the country pursue a sort of masked dance, invoking by words and gestures a western constitutional order, and giving to the entire world the impression, convincing only to the non-initiated, that Burundi has renounced its history and transformed itself into a European-type constitutional monarchy.

Bujumbura was no more than a town at the time, and the country had a mere handful of secondary schools and university-educated nationals. The circle of people who competed for power was mainly composed of Ganwa, Tutsi close to the royal court, and some high-caste Hutu. A fierce rivalry emerged among families of Ganwa, continuing at least a century of antagonism (ibid.). The king's authority, already weakened by decades of colonialism, was insufficient to resolve these recurring crises. Over time, these fights for power began to acquire an ethnic tone. Four years after independence, the king was deposed by the army, and almost three decades of rule by low-caste Tutsi military from Bururi began.

There was, during those years, still no major social demand for democracy. Laely, who did his research in the late 1980s, writes:

> Current relationships between rulers and ruled in Burundi are still influenced by the old monarchical model of domination in many respects. Access to the state and its infrastructures is perceived as a special favour, not least since the services provided are still not generalised and often distributed arbitrarily or at random. [...] The rulers of today are perceived to a lesser degree than in the past as benefactors, albeit still as the most efficient potential protectors. [...] The peasants look upon the achievements of those in authority – and the latter include the intercessors in the post-colonial state – as the equivalent out-

come of their own services rendered beforehand, and sometimes even as generous favours. This helps to explain why relations to superiors are actively sought, and not perceived or felt to be oppressive, despite or even because of the implicated arbitrariness.

In short, what ordinary Burundians wanted was not democracy but a system – or people – that delivered, as in being effective, recognizable, acceptable.

Under those circumstances, what Westerners call corruption, or clientelism, was to ordinary Burundians normal, understandable, and uncontested. It displayed predictability and it provided rewards to those who were good at it, for both elites and ordinary people. Hence, for decades, all new entrants into positions of importance in the country were socialized into this system, its rules and demands very clear to them – ambiguous or incomprehensible only to the outsider, who focuses exclusively on the formal institutions of the state (see Chabal and Daloz 1999).

During the decades of military rule from 1966 to 1993, major changes started taking place in how the state related to the citizens, which eventually led to the destruction of this system. One change was the weakening of the checks and balances that had characterized the pre-colonial proto-state. Commune and *colline* borders were redrawn so they did not fit traditional *chef* and *sous-chef* areas anymore; the institution of *bashingantahe* was weakened; central state coercive power was exercised raw and naked to defend the status quo, as attested above all by the mass killings of Hutu in 1972.

Unlike the former kingdom, which found legitimacy in shared religious values and symbols, a dictatorship of low-caste Tutsi had little to justify itself by. The successive military regimes and the single party they managed primarily sought control, and secondarily legitimacy. For the former, brutal violence was used whenever necessary; for the rest, the regimes sought to supervise and control every aspect of social life. The state and the single party both had structures reaching down all the way to the *collines* and everyone with a position in the former had to be member of

73

the latter. Local state and party institutions were not institutions of citizenship but of control, and, for those who managed to become part of them, of individual advancement. The regimes also sought to construct two pillars of legitimacy: nationalism and development. UPRONA adhered to an ideology of nationalism that had the added convenience of hiding the disproportionate power held by a small group of people (Lemarchand 1996). Prince Louis Rwagasore, the young, modern, charismatic politician shot to death before coming to power, was the ideal symbol for the party, trying to reach into the past while being ruled by people with no past. Development – the ideology of material progress and individual advancement – was the other pillar, probably more important to and successful with foreigners than with most rural Burundians. Development projects were used as tools to continue clientelism at the local level.

By the late 1970s, the state had become a giant machine sucking income out of the (mainly Hutu) rural poor toward the (mainly Tutsi) urban rich. Corruption grew, and with it disincentives against investment. This system could last only as long as it produced the goods, i.e. as long as it managed to create some development throughout the country and to generate enough jobs for aspirants to power to share in the pie. But economic growth slowed down to a trickle, and intra-elite political competition began rising. Popular unhappiness started growing as well – primarily among Hutu intellectuals, who felt socially excluded, but also among Tutsi. But there is more.

We said earlier that what Westerners call corruption was to ordinary Burundians normal. True, but there *are* borders – lines that can be redrawn, but which denote real differences most everyone recognizes.[5] Increasingly, the types of abuse of power that many politicians and administrators engaged in went beyond what could be justified or recognized by ordinary Burundians: 'people perceive that forms of corruption no longer rooted in a moral economy of kinship are on the rise' (Smith 2007). Showing great deference to people of authority is a traditional norm, indeed, and it is not difficult for a Burundian farmer to enact these behaviors – the shuffling, the downcast eyes, the left hand on top of the right arm – when asking for services she would legally deserve to access as a citizen, but when that same administrator abuses his power to capture lands of her family, he has gone beyond what is mutually legitimate, and they both know it. When teachers require sex with female students to let them pass, or when employers do the same to hire, this not only runs counter to the modesty Burundians pride themselves on; it is also perceived as a clear abuse of power.

In addition, the values of the modern state – even if that state was in practice subverted – did slowly spread throughout Burundi. While Burundi's imported 'modern' state was always more a façade than a reality, it did bring with it new values and new rhetoric. There *were* laws on the books, and sometimes they *were* applied correctly. There were increasingly well-trained young people who brought with them a desire for another way of working. Foreigners and aid agencies did bring with them different discourses and tried to function according to different rules. The official rhetoric of the state of equality and progress and rationality – mainly designed for international consumption – did trickle down, and the contrast between these proclamations and reality became clearer. But although individual people may be more aware of some of these concepts, that does not mean they are as a society ready to challenge the status quo. To quote Laely one last time:

> The attitudes adopted by mainstream peasantry can most aptly be summarised as pragmatic and realistic: by succumbing more frequently to actions taken by the state than ever feeling to be 'involved', they adapt to given circumstances. Experiencing their powerlessness, they try to align themselves with the powerful as best they can. Although new concepts, such as equality of opportunity and equal rights, are not unknown, most peasants continue to let themselves be guided by traditional patterns of behaviour and values. Their reactions are in general much more often personal than collective. In short, the strategies adopted by

most towards the state can be described as strongly 'defensive' and 'individual.'

The civil war provided the final blow to this system. It laid bare the system's illegitimacy and its total ineffectiveness, as well as the fact that nobody in power gave a damn about the needs of the poor. It weaned ordinary Burundians off of any belief in the old system.

The level of suffering during the war was enormous. Burundi, already one of the world's poorest countries, became dramatically poorer still. Almost every family lost its assets, and the state did nothing about it – nor, for that matter, did the rebels. Stuck in their camps like cattle – refugee camps, IDP camps, *camps de regroupement* – and dependent on small amounts of outside charity, Burundians were profoundly humiliated by the war. And the politicians, in the meantime, were never to be seen: they did not suffer like the people they claimed to represent; their rhetoric of ethnic solidarity meant nothing in daily life. Burundians became angry – and it is this anger I heard in so many conversations. How different their voices sounded from twenty years earlier, when I worked in rural Burundi!

Some people described that new-found assertiveness. One of the most interesting was a priest who had been in the same rural convent for eight years. He told me that in the recent electoral campaign he had been struck by how people were more willing to give their opinions and ask critical questions. He felt this was a result of the shock of the war, which destroyed the status quo. He repeated thrice to me that for him the war was a 'necessary evil.'

Another important change that happened as a result of the war is that the state lost its monopoly on information and organization. Until the early 1990s, Burundi was an extremely closed society. Most citizens lived on their *collines* and hardly ever moved away from them. The prime source of information was the government-owned radio. There were no Burundian NGOs, no critical voices beyond whispered rumors, no legal opposition parties, no independent think tanks. The war knocked intellectuals out of their lethargy: it made them suffer and made them angry; it closed off jobs and forced them to become more dynamic. At the same time, the capacity of the state to control everything declined dramatically. Initially, a lot of Burundi's emerging media outlets and NGOs were extremely biased and partial, but over time professionalism increased and new ones came into being, and smart young Burundian men and women built, piece by little piece, a totally different, pluralist civil society.

This civil society has now known a decade of growth and maturation, and it is a force to be reckoned with. It is admittedly still strongly Bujumbura-based, although outreach beyond the capital is growing. Some important civil society organizations now have a significant presence beyond Bujumbura: they are principally human rights NGOs, but also some dealing with conflict resolution and development. But far and away the most impact beyond the capital is made by the many quality independent radio stations such as RPA and Isanganiro. This means that there is a breadth of information available to all citizens now, often critical – including a lot of coverage of corruption.

Conclusion

Transitions like Burundi's are moments of uncertainty. New institutions are developed, new entrants occupy positions on the central stage, new laws are written. Minds have been changed, hearts have been hardened, expectations shattered, networks dissolved. Much of this is not good news, but some of it contains seeds for change. At the same time, the old has not just totally disappeared: those power relations, expectations, values, and networks are still there, although they have been affected in many ways. There are factors pushing toward change, and factors pushing toward the return of the status quo, and it is not obvious which way things will go. This duality of change and continuity exists at the top and at the bottom of society.

Ordinary Burundians have become far more critical toward the state and the powers that be as a result of the war. They ask more questions, they do not unquestioningly follow leaders anymore, they voice their displeasure more easily. Reflexive ethnicity is weaker than before: many Burundians realize it has not served them and wish to move beyond it. But ethnic division has not suddenly lost all its salience: there is too much pain, too much memory, and humans are not lizards who can overnight shed one skin in favor of another. And most ordinary Burundians have long learned to distrust '*Leta*' (the Kirundi word for the state, which includes the international community) and to make themselves as small and invisible as possible before it, asking for favors rather than rights (Pouligny 2006: 103, 109).

As shown in the previous chapter, the overwhelming major-ity of Burundians do not demand the Western institutions of democracy (the only ones the international community is capable of recognizing or conceiving of). They care far more for security and minimal development than for elections or human rights laws. At the same time, they deeply desire equity, respect, an end to corruption. Burundians have a language, a set of values, to describe better governance with, and it is the language of the institution of *bashingantahe*. A deep adherence to values of truth, justice, non-discrimination appeared everywhere in our conversations. While at first sight similar to Western concepts of human rights and good governance, this *bashingantahe*-inspired notion of respect is less focused on 'right structures' and more on 'good people.'

But new institutions with the potential to facilitate change *have* come into being as a result of the war. The press has become diverse, courageous, often in touch with the countryside and the lives of ordinary people. More NGOs, foreign and national, work closely with the people and can create opportunities for local innovation.

Political change *is* possible in post-war Burundi. The future is not fixed – it is neither a guaranteed march toward progress, nor an inevitable decline to the situation of before. Things are contin-gent, and individuals – Hussain Radjabu, for example, for the two years he led the CNDD/FDD – can have profound impacts.

What is the role of international aid in all this? The international community was very successful in supporting the transition to peace in Burundi: it facilitated the negotiations, and supported the implementation of their results both through carrots (support to temporarily bloated institutions; private guards for returning politicians; promises of more development aid; leadership seminars at the highest levels; early support for DDR) and sticks (threats of reductions in aid; united diplomatic pressure). Once the transition was successful – i.e. most of the hostilities were ended and, especially, once peaceful elections were held – the situation became a lot more complicated.[6] No longer did the international community share the same clear goal; the mechanisms for donor coordination became weaker (in part because the newly elected government itself wanted to weaken them – hence its attack against the UN leadership); the usual disjointed system reemerged.

This system understands pretty much nothing of the dynamics of political change I documented in this chapter. Democracy, good governance, rule of law, justice – all are on the agenda, but none of these is rooted in a fine understanding of the specifics of Burundi. Donors continue to profess totally unrealistic goals – what Pritchett and Woolcock (2004) so nicely call 'skipping straight to Denmark,' without clear intermediary goals (Ottaway 2002), a fine sense of the system they are intervening in (Pouligny 2006), or any discussion of what they will abstain from intervening in (Uvin 2004).

Indeed, donors, in Burundi and elsewhere, seem incapable of understanding politics or acting politically. There are important processes that can lead to peace, the expression of citizenship, and the learning of democracy in Burundian society. But donors fail to understand them or to act on them. They simply copy products, but do not support processes. This worked reasonably well when it came to the transition, which consisted of a set of clearly defined products: demobilization of soldiers, creation of a transitional government – any government – for a number of months, organization of elections by a specific deadline, etc. But it works a lot less well once this easy phase is out of the way, and sustainable, locally owned institutions need to take root in Burundian society. At that point, the 'product vision' becomes largely irrelevant: it may be writable, subcontractable, manageable and spendable, but it is also overwhelmingly irrelevant.

Most of the democracy and governance work supported by the international community does not involve any opportunities for the exercise of real power or learning by Burundian citizens, and is thus easily manipulated by political elites and insiders. Too busy copying their own institutions, typing endless reports and sitting in interminable meetings, disconnected from the reality of urban and rural life, saturated by a constant stream of missions, expert reports, assessments, workshops, and indicators, donors fall back on the standard solutions and products. Recipient governments and elites much prefer this product-centered approach to governance, for it is much easier to sabotage or appropriate.

Take the decentralization policy – a favorite of the development community in Burundi for close to three decades now, and hence one every local insider knows how to play like a well-strung tambour! The decentralization law is entirely set up to create the least possible bottom-up dynamic and the maximum amount of centralized control. But the donors love decentralization, and masses of money flows into it – in the name of service delivery, good governance, or conflict resolution. And so donors do again all the same old things they always did: lots of training – the same people over and over receiving training from different agencies on the same subject, politely collecting their per diems; some general campaigns to educate the masses in how the new institutions in theory work; and of course the building of buildings everywhere. Most of this is entirely irrelevant to the real potential for citizen-driven democratization in Burundi. It will produce nothing in the way of citizenship or true democracy.[7]

5 | Hard work and prostitution: the capitalist ethos in crisis[1]

In this chapter, we bring together the answers to questions that deal with economic well-being. This was by far the largest section of our conversations. We asked people both to *describe* their own lives, plans, dreams, and support networks, and to *analyze* long-term trends, social mobility, and gender differences. No one single vision presented itself: people's analyses diverged, according to their objective circumstances (whether they were rural or urban, women or men, migrants or not) and subjective factors (their personal values and trajectories).

There is a growing literature about the economic dimension of the post-conflict agenda (Collier 2003; Addison 2003). What should be the economic priorities of post-conflict countries? Is economic liberalization after war a bad idea? Is economic growth possible without major prior investment in public infrastructure, or without major improvements in governance first? Should conflict resolution concerns be mainstreamed into economic projects (multi-ethnic cooperatives, for example, or positive discrimination measures to combat horizontal inequality) or should economic growth be the prime aim? Most of these concerns are very macro-oriented and expert-based. Here, we present the voices of some of the millions of ordinary Burundians who struggle each day to eke out a meager existence for themselves and their children. After twelve years of war, how do they survive? How do they see the future?

Changes since time of parents: long-term trends

We first present the results to the question: 'how is your life different from the life of your parents?' This was a way for us to encourage people to analyze long-term development trends.

It is also an entirely open-ended question: it did not specify any field of human life. People could discuss trends in the economic, social, personal, or collective realm – and they did.

Unsurprisingly, the large majority of people, especially in rural areas, thought the long-term conditions of life had deteriorated (same results in MINIPLAN 2006: 11). Ruhororo and Kamenge were most negative in their outlook. These are both places where nearly all people consider themselves to be on a downward slope in life (a fact corroborated by their answers to many other questions). Yet these are very different places. Ruhororo is totally rural, Kamenge urban; Ruhororo's IDP camp, where most (but not all) interviews took place, is fully inhabited by Tutsi, whereas Kamenge is almost exclusively Hutu. What these two places share, however, is that they have been among the very worst hit by the war for many years, and full of people who carry deep personal traumas – and nothing has changed since the end of the war. The continued impact of the war, then, can clearly be seen in these answers.

Almost all people in rural areas gave us reasons for why their lives were not as good as their parents'. They identified three roughly equal factors: the war, climate change, and population growth. I expected the war to be the prime factor causing a deterioration in people's lives, and, indeed, in conversation after conversation, people detailed to us the many losses they had suffered during the war: in order of frequency, these include theft of animals, theft of other possessions, destruction of property, being forced to flee, losing years of schooling, death of family members, permanent injury. I did not expect population pressure and climate change, however, to be mentioned as frequently as the war. Note that when people talk about climate change, they are referring to the frequent droughts that occurred during the last decade in Burundi. Many people talked about lack of land – logical in a country where 57 percent of households have less than one hectare to live off (ibid.: 42). All this demonstrates that even in countries at war, there is more going on than war. War may capture the attention, dominate the political discourse, and

TABLE 5.1 General trends

	Busiga	Ruhororo	Nyanza-Lac	Musaga	Kamenge	Bwiza	Other urban	Total
Deterioration	30	56	24	13	15	6	10	154
Improvement	13	2	18	19	1	5	16	74

its resolution may be a *sine qua non* for meaningful change, but it is *not* the full story of life, and people know it.

About one third of our interviewees discussed *improvements*, rather than deteriorations, when they compared their lives to their parents'. This is far beyond what I had expected, given the fact that Burundi had come out of twelve years of almost constant violence and economic decline. This was especially the case in parts of the city, where this type of response constituted almost half of all answers. And many of the people who answered positively were not the richest in society.

In Ngozi province, more than half of the (few) positive answers came from women, who told us that they were more independent now. This may be related to a major and rather successful gender empowerment project there by an American NGO, CARE. In Nyanza-Lac, about one third of the people saw positive trends – by far the highest in the rural areas we worked in. People (especially older ones) here often told us that they lived more *modern* lives – they have better clothes and wash more, can buy a broader range of products at the local market, have more free time and are more independently minded.[2] In this commune, there is generally a sense of moderate optimism as to the economic future – that it is possible to make it, to feed oneself decently, to give better education to one's children, if one just works hard and smartly. There is more land here, and more trade as well, than in Ngozi province. Part of this optimism may also be related to the fact that Nyanza-Lac is a land of migrants and returnees. Eighty percent of our interviewees were recent returnees from Tanzania or from IDP camps in Burundi. These are all people who have recent bad memories and who were very pleased to start a normal life again, in a place with visible economic potential.

But the two groups that stand out for the high proportion of positive answers are the rich in Bujumbura and the people from Musaga. Both these places are overwhelmingly urban and Tutsi, as well as disproportionately composed of migrants.[3] This suggests a very important political fact in Burundi, namely that those who are upwardly mobile in the country are mainly Tutsi, and they are generally a group that is more positive in its outlook on life than most other people, for they have a sense of forward momentum. This seems to persist even though the Tutsi as a group have lost political hegemony. In other words, while political power may have shifted in Burundi, deeper social and economic processes – resulting from historical differences in access to education and social networks – have not yet. And hence, even at the end of a war that they, from an ethno-political perspective, objectively lost (and they know it), many Tutsi may still be benefiting in the economic realm from the advantages that the previous system conferred on them.

This is surely not unique to Burundi: El Salvador and South Africa immediately come to mind as situations where similar dynamics occurred. What these cases share is that their transition to war from peace results from negotiations, in which a formerly dominant group loses its monopoly on political power but keeps many of its economic assets. This may help to promote their buy-in to the political transition and thus have a stabilizing effect on it – although it may of course produce the inverse effect on the people on the other side of the social equation, in this case the Hutu, who find they did not gain as much as hoped for from the struggle. As a result, in Burundi assessments of the recent transition are not purely ethnic – even though the war itself was fought along ethnic lines. Hutu from Kamenge are generally less pleased with life after war than Tutsi from Musaga; similarly, Hutu may admire Buyoya more than Tutsi do, and Nkurunziza is popular among many Tutsi.

This also throws light on debates about horizontal inequality, i.e. when economic differences overlap with ethnic ones (Stewart 2000). First, aggregate data on rural poverty in Burundi demonstrate that average incomes of Hutu and Tutsi are roughly equal there; it is only at the level of the upper class that Tutsi had major advantages. This observation is often taken by Great Lakes specialists to disprove the notion of horizontal inequality – Hutu and Tutsi are equally poor, they argue, and it is only a small group (no more than 1 percent of society, really) of politicians, military and bureaucrats who are well off. But this underestimates the social facts of mobility and expectations: more Tutsi managed to escape the rural world than Hutu did, and this makes an enormous socio-political difference. Second, horizontal inequality is sticky – it does not change easily. When the political system changes the persistence of horizontal inequality creates a more mixed system, with a likely stabilizing impact. Horizontal inequality, in short, is a crucial phenomenon in many societies.

Education

Education is the issue that came up most in our conversations about how (young) people try to make it in life. It is at the heart of individual social mobility and family strategies for survival.

Let me begin with some data: I kept information on the educational attainment of almost all of the 388 persons I interviewed. In Ngozi province, the average educational attainment was between fifth and sixth grade. In Nyanza-Lac this dropped to fourth grade. Among the poor in the city of Bujumbura, educational level was no higher than in Nyanza-Lac. Among the rich, it was eleventh grade – vastly higher. Generally, as elsewhere in the world, our data show a strong correlation between educational attainment and income level, both in rural and urban areas. Of course, this tells us nothing about the direction of causality. Note the interesting anomaly that, in rural areas, the educational attainment of well-off farmers is not higher, and in one case is actually lower, than that of the poorer farmers (also observed in MINIPLAN 2006: 35). Our interviews suggest that this may be due to the fact that the minority of well-off farmers value education less, for they are confident in the capacity of their children to live off agriculture and they prefer to maintain a traditionally valued lifestyle.

Another fascinating question is to disaggregate educational achievement data by group in terms of how the war affected them. The results are surprising. First, in the countryside, most people are pretty much equal – whether you fail primary school finals at age twelve before the war or at age fifteen because you missed

TABLE 5.2 Education per category, in years, by region

	All	Urban	Rural
People who stayed at home	7.3	10.3	5.0
IDPs	5.4	6.1	5.0
Repatriated refugees	5.9	8.2[1]	5.2
Child soldiers	3.2	4.2	2.4
Adult ex-combatants	6.9	8.0 (6.7)[2]	5.4
Migrants	7.5	8.0	3.2[3]
TOTAL	6.5	8.1	5.0

Notes: 1. N = 5 only. 2. If we take away five career FAB soldiers, the average falls to 6.7. 3. N = 6 only.

three years of schooling owing to the war makes little difference in the long run. In the city, however, all people who did not stay at home – all people who were forcibly displaced, or who joined the fighting – are significantly worse off than those who stayed at home. For city dwellers, then, it is clear that not having had to flee has constituted a major educational bonus.[4] There are pockets of exceptions as well. In the IDP camp in Ruhororo, for example, we found a very high educational level for young women – ninth grade on average for our group of interviewees. With little agricultural occupation and the close availability of a recently built school, families sent their kids to school, and, as is the case almost everywhere, girls did extremely well when given the opportunity.

If anybody has really missed out on education as a result of the war, it is child soldiers, who have by far the lowest educational achievement of any group. This legacy is, however, less dramatic than may appear at first. The differences with non-combatant civilians of their age are generally not enormous (see too Taouti-Cherif 2006: 25), for the large majority of poor people in Burundi suffered from low access to education during and before the war. At the same time, as we will show below, education makes a serious difference in Burundians' life only if they reach at least tenth grade. Whether they have four years of education while others have six years does not really make that much of a difference – you remain on the farm or in the informal sector regardless (Uvin 2007b).

A few more words about urban migrants. We have data for sixty-six of them, all of whom had moved from the interior to Bujumbura during their own lifetime, almost all without their family. Their educational attainment is much higher than the average rural educational attainment – than that of the peers they left behind, in other words. Actually, migrants are better educated than their non-migrant peers at all levels of income, although the difference is especially striking at higher levels. This clearly documents the well-known phenomenon of rural–urban brain drain. But disaggregation is in order here too. This group is composed of at least two subgroups: those who came to the city to study – mostly at university or in other post-secondary training, but some also in secondary school – and those who came to the city *after* they became '*déscolarisés*,' in search of income opportunities. It is of course especially the former group which jacks up the average educational attainment of the migrant category. The latter group is not very different at all: for them it is not studies, but dynamism, or personal networks, which explains their migration fate.

As said earlier, education is the issue that came up most in conversations. For Burundians, clearly, it is the best if not the only way out of farming (a trend in much of Africa; Hyden 2006: 149). The juxtaposition between education and agriculture – and more broadly between education and the rural life – came through in hundreds of conversations. A smattering of quotes will illustrate this:

> People with education have more job opportunities, especially if they have high school degree. So they can have a job and live independently of the life in the *collines*. (Twenty-year-old farmer, five years of schooling, Busiga)

> If you don't study, the only opportunity is to cultivate ten hours a

day under a hot sun, every day of the year. (Twenty-eight-year-old civil servant, one year of university, Ruhororo)

I admire people who have studied and have a degree. They do not have to pass their entire days cultivating, they earn money and help their families escape poverty. I regret not having continued my studies. (Thirty-year-old widow, finished primary school)

It will come as no surprise that many people told us that the prime determinant for quality of life of young people is whether they have done further studies. This held for both men and women (out of fifty-six times education was mentioned in this context, for example, it applied twenty-seven times to men and twenty-nine times to women).

Education means you are not stuck anymore in the prison that rural life represents for many people. This means that for people the investment in education is mainly worth it if one gets to the end of the process. The economic benefits of education are much more of an all-or-nothing nature – not a gradual process – than is usually acknowledged. It is not as if each year of additional schooling makes Burundians one thirteenth better off. Rather, once one passes the level at which one can read and write there is a long plateau of few increased personal quality-of-life gains, and then a dramatic increase after tenth grade, and especially at completion of high school. This is why so many people talked to us about education *'jusqu'au diplome'* – until the diploma – for that is where education pays off.

Burundians' strong attachment to education may be due to political factors as well. One of the key ways in which social exclusion was produced and reproduced in pre-war Burundi was through highly unequal access to education, and especially the type of education that matters, namely secondary and tertiary (Jackson 2000). The most violent form thereof was what Lemarchand (1996) has labeled the 'selective genocide' of 1972, which entailed the almost complete elimination of all educated Hutu in Burundi. For many years, Hutu parents feared sending their children to school, so intense was the trauma of those events. Unequal access to education was also reproduced through unequal schooling infrastructures, with a heavy regional bias toward Bujumbura and Bururi province, the two places where the elite in power were most present. Nyanza-Lac, for example, while adjacent to Bururi and, until the late 1980s, part of Bururi province, had not a single secondary school until 1996, well into the civil war! In a country where all the desirable positions – in the state, the aid system, the small private enterprise sector, the superior echelons of the army – require higher education, this meant a de facto exclusion from opportunities for advancement. Even now, the majority of the 4,000 students enrolled in the national university are Tutsi (Economist Intelligence Unit 2006). Note that, for decades, the international development community invested massively in education in Burundi without ever addressing this dramatic social exclusion.

Under those circumstances, it comes as no surprise that the very first decision of President Nkurunziza was to announce universal free primary education. This was a smart political move, demonstrating that from now on 'the system' in Burundi has changed, and all Burundians will find their place in the country. It is possible that, in this political context, part of the massive adhesion to education we observed in our interviews is explained by a catch-up movement. This is confirmed by another observation: when we asked young people themselves for their own plans in life, we got by far the highest number of 'education' answers in Kamenge, Burundi's radical Hutu neighborhood par excellence. On the other hand, this is emphatically *not* the only factor explaining the importance of education to Burundians, for it occurred pretty much equally among Hutu and Tutsi, rich and poor, born from highly educated parents or not, rural or urban, male or female.

All secondary school students we interviewed (often well into their twenties) felt enormous pressure to perform and identified deeply with being a student. For these youths, studying hard is the only shot they have at lifting themselves, and their families, out of a deeply uncertain future. As one nineteen-year-old ninth grade student in Ruhororo told us, 'In the camp, I saw many young men who abandoned school because of lack of money, and that tormented me. I told myself that if this were to happen one day to me, I would become crazy.' They study night after night by candlelight, until their eyes give up – we met many people who had to abandon their studies because their eyes couldn't take it anymore.

Little do they know how hard it is for educated young people in the city, competing against thousands of others, to find a decent job, especially if they have no connections. Some of the unhappiest people I met were young men in Bujumbura, after all these years of sacrifice, desperately looking for a job, month after month after month. Some don't even manage to find the money to print their final theses, and will thus never get their degrees. They worked so hard, got so close, and then they still find the door closed. It is my impression that these are not people who are inclined to violence and self-destruction: they are too serious for that, they have given too much, they want to belong to the system more than anything else. And so they doggedly keep on going, asking around, trying to ingratiate themselves with more powerful people (including any foreigners they can get to meet), waiting for the day they will get a job, any job, anywhere.

Education is a lottery, especially for the poor – and it is an expensive one at that. When harvests are bad, when people are sick, when assets are stolen, when families are forced to flee, education is interrupted if not ended altogether.[5] And if poverty, sickness, or violence don't cut short education, then the extremely tough schooling system will: pass rates of less than 25 percent are normal. In the rural world, less than 9 percent of children go on to secondary school; in the city of Bujumbura that is 37 percent (MINIPLAN 2006: 10).

Since the overwhelming majority of the rural youth never gets even close to finishing their education *'jusqu'au diplome,'* the issue becomes: what to do next? The current answer for most Burundian youth is: nothing. There is essentially no 'plan B.'

Thus, it comes as no surprise that this research uncovered a profound and widespread desire for vocational training, especially in the northern communes (Sommers 2006b: 15). Person after person, in our conversations in these two communes, spontaneously brought up vocational training, whether talking about their own lives or about what to do for youth in general.

Migration

The communal development plan of Musaga indicates that 40 percent of all households migrated there during the war – my sample has an even higher proportion. Yet we know almost nothing about migration in Burundi. We have no idea at all of actual numbers, and neither are there any social science studies on the matter. This is related to the image that prevails about Burundi as an exclusively rural country. A major 2007 GoB/UN document prepared for the Peace Building Commission, for example, starts with the statement that '95% of all Burundians live off agriculture.' This is far from true but it is believed by all. Here is what we learned from listening to the people in both a major out-migration area (Ngozi province) and the country's main in-migration area, Bujumbura city.

The rural world In our interviews in poor, overpopulated Ngozi province, young men and young women told us over and over that they would love to migrate to the city, for there is not enough land anymore, not enough to eat, no opportunities to earn money. A major reason young men migrate – or desire to do so – is in the hope of saving enough money to build a house, pay bride wealth, and get married. Indeed, our interviews suggest that many rural men migrate to the city precisely to prepare for marriage. Married men who do not already work in the city rarely migrate there (it is different for those who live in towns surrounding cities).

> After the death of my parents and oldest brother, I took care of the siblings. In 1997, I came to Bujumbura to do different jobs and then I managed to buy my own bike and I started doing

taxi-vélo. I have done this job since 2002 and it allows me to have everything I need. I managed to build a house and I married because of my work. I also managed to buy three goats and five parcels of land to cultivate. I think that with God's help I will manage the development I wished for when I came to the city. (Twenty-six-year-old migrant, Musaga)

I am saving some money to buy a couple of cows. After that, I will seek a wife. I am busy building a house with a tile roof in my *colline* to prepare my marriage. (Twenty-year-old male migrant, Musaga)

I want to build a house [in his *colline*] from next summer onwards, and afterwards I intend to marry. I think two people are better than one and we can unite our strengths to assure our projects. (Nineteen-year-old male migrant, Musaga)

The number of young people who told us they were *not* interested in migrating, for life was good as it was, was less than 10 percent of the total in both northern communes. As Ruhororo was deeply struck by the war whereas Busiga was mainly spared, this seems largely independent of the war.

I asked many young people in the countryside why they were staying there, rather than going to the city. Their main answer was economic in nature: the risk is too high, and they are too poor to make it in the city. While the city has the potential for a better life, that result is far from certain. Ultimately, the countryside is stable and predictable – you know what you have, *even if it is not much*. At home, you have food and a support network. Life is hard, but at least it is predictably hard and you are not alone. Listen to this nineteen-year-old returned former child soldier:

I am able to see friends in the *centre de negoce*, and they are able to give me a bit of money for breakfast, or let me unload merchandise for two hundred francs. Going to the city is not interesting, because few people know me there. Who could help me and give me money in times of need?

Other people argue that, sure, you can make more money in the city, but life is more expensive there as well, as you need to buy everything. Others still pointed out that to make it in the city you need to have start-up capital and know someone who can help you: in the absence of that, it is much too risky to go to the city. As this twenty-four-year-old man from Busiga said: 'I stay here because there is more stability in the *colline*. Even though I am poor, I can go to friends or relatives to get food or money. This is not the case in the city, plus, in order to get there, I must start with some capital.' Or this eighteen-year-old IDP in Ruhororo: 'Going to the city is like a lottery, if you don't know someone who supports you, and helps you find work.' In short, for many people, it seems the risk–benefit or the cost–benefit ratio is too low.

A few young people told us they would love to go to the city but their responsibilities keep them home. Sick parents, too much work, the need to take care of younger siblings, the fact of being the oldest son – all these factors were invoked to explain why a person could not migrate even if he wanted to.

A larger group of people gave as reason for not migrating the fact that the city is a place of sin, of temptation, of danger. Many of them were older, talking about their attitude toward their children. This is how a fifty-one-year-old farmer saw it: 'Girls here do fieldwork and household work. When they start to have bad behavior, they migrate to the city to find work there.' Some young people copy the values of their elders. This twenty-nine-year-old-man, for example, said: 'I think young people who go to the city are lazy people who flee from cultivating the land. They want to go to the city, thinking that life will be very easy.' It is clear that part of the general atmosphere of the countryside is still opposed to urban migration. Many of the migrants do rather well – certainly no worse than had they stayed put. At the same time, an image persists in which those young people who leave for the city are the ones who don't fit in, who are too lazy to work hard, who are tempted by the easy life and want glittery things. In short, they are cultural and social outcasts, not responsible, obedient, well-educated children.

This image is especially pronounced in the case of young women who go to the city. With the exception of those girls who pursue their studies, migrant women are generally described in terms of laziness, moral weakness, and, especially, sexual loss of innocence. Young people themselves subscribed to this image. A twenty-four-year-old woman told us: 'Those who have bad behavior are the ones who migrate to the cities. Why? they don't have the same esprit, they are not satisfied with their natural life, they look for other means to survive and this leads to bad behavior.' This twenty-two-year-old displaced man presented the complete picture:

> It is worse for girls than boys, because when they spend some time in the city they start to acculturate: they wear pants or miniskirts and use make-up. As a result, most of them start to forget themselves and maintain relations with boys in the city and fall pregnant. When they come back to the countryside, they are marginalized in every way: way of dressing, having an illegitimate child. They don't even manage to feed their children the right way, and they die of malnutrition. When the child dies, it is very hard for the girl because people tell her that they cannot bury the child if they don't know the father. Other girls prefer to abort their pregnancy, but when they are identified, they are caught and imprisoned. Those young women who did not find husbands in the city end up coming back to the countryside. But who would ask her hand in the countryside with her marginal behavior? People think that she has already forgotten the work in the field and she is considered lazy.

This ideology is not surprising. In all cultures, women are the embodiment of traditional values: home, community, the nation. Their chastity is prized above all, and fears about unbridled female sexuality abound – according to some scholars, this is all the more so in wartime (Rajasingham-Senanyake 2001; Giles and Hyndman 2004). I believe that the deep connection between migration and loss of female sexual innocence is not so much a statement of fact (although there are of course cases where it is factually correct) as the result of a double cultural dynamic. One aspect is that women who migrate move beyond the boundaries of social expectations about gender roles. Negative images about their sexuality are intended to prevent this from happening. Old people are the ones who presented these images most frequently and clearly. But the fact that a number of young people invoked these very images as their reason not to migrate as well demonstrates that there is a deeper and widespread ideological support basis for these images. But there is more. We should not forget that a similar aspersion existed about young men as well – while it did not focus on their sexuality, it did put into doubt their uprightness. At a deeper level, then, this whole imagery is a reflection of the fear that exists in the rural world about it losing its character, about the ongoing social change. These images reflect the resistance to change and decline of a centuries-old culture that centers on agriculture – the land, the animals, the seasons; the social relations, proverbs, and expectations associated with that. In short, what we see at work here is the resistance created by a combination of rural and gendered values.

The case of the Ruhororo IDP camp was especially interesting in that regard. It seemed that, every single time the issue of female migration came up, it was associated with the words 'unwanted pregnancy.' In almost the same words, everyone told us that 'girls who go to the city will return pregnant and unmarried, and their children suffer from *kwashiorkor* [malnutrition caused by insufficient protein intake].' No other path was possible or conceivable, it seems. It is our hypothesis that the extremely common attachment to the most rigid traditional image is the result of the very high level of frustrations with their fate among men there.

Bujumbura city The migrants I interviewed in the city had come there for different reasons and by different paths. One can distinguish four groups. First are those who migrated before the war, often in pursuit of higher education. Many of them came from the south, principally Bururi. They are mostly the elite class of society. They are often Tutsi, male, well educated, and older. The other three groups I encountered are composed of younger people who migrated to Bujumbura during the war years. Three prime motivations drove them: to continue their studies, to look for work, or to escape the violence and the war.

The last group contains a number of people, Tutsi and Hutu, who suffered horribly from the war. They did not come to Bujumbura as part of a plan but simply had to flee; often their immediate family is dead and they depend on the kindness of remote family or strangers; they have little education and no capital to start a business. If they are women, they often have stories of sexual abuse behind them. They are among the people who suffered most of those we met during our months talking to ordinary Burundians. They are also among the poorest people we interviewed in the city. There are many of them in Kamenge (coming from Bujumbura rural) but also in Musaga.

The two other groups share a lot. They both came to Bujumbura deliberately. They are both upwardly mobile, even if only slightly or only potentially. They are often poor, living under tough circumstances, working hard to survive, frustrated by their poverty and afraid of the future – but, nevertheless, they have a sense of momentum, of potential, if things work out.

One of the most striking research results was the significant difference that exists between urban immigrants and urban people born in the city. Among the latter, anomie is much higher, and the deep sense of capitalist ethic was expressed much less frequently. More of the young people who spent all their days hanging out at the *ligala* were urban born. More of those who had no plans or hope for the future were urban born. More of those who joined the rebels – or the self-defense forces – were urban born. More of the young men who had children out of wedlock were urban born. In our interviews, the urban-born young people were not poorer than the rural-born ones, so objective facts do not explain this. What differentiates them, I believe, are subjective factors: whom they compare themselves to, and what trajectory they see their lives as being on. In simple terms, the rural-to-urban migrants compare themselves to their countryside fellow men, and, of course, to how they were before they came to the city. While they are by all standards poor – and they know it: it is not ignorance which drives this – they consider themselves relatively better off than before, or than their rural peers, and many of them also have the sense that, with luck and hard work, they can improve their fate further. Urban-born boys are in a very different situation. Many of them have been distinctly downwardly mobile, as the economy has slowed over the years, as households have fallen apart, as their own parents have not managed to live up to their responsibilities. At the same time, their comparison group is the urban rich – not the rural poor, with whom they have no contact. For them, it is the lives behind the high walls in the *quartiers des chefs* which constitute their comparison level, the big cars with tinted windows speeding by which they wish to possess, the well-dressed and drunk people coming out of nightclubs with sexy women on their arms who they aspire to be.

There is probably a third element at work as well in explaining the difference between urban-born and immigrant young men in Bujumbura, namely the lower social control in the city compared to the countryside. In the rural world, children, when not in school, cannot go far: there is always someone around who knows them, and there is little mischief to be had in any case. In the city, clearly, there are many more temptations and opportunities. As a result, urban-born young men fall more easily into trajectories of nihilism and drugs.

Social mobility

We asked all our interviewees what the situation of people their own age was, and if people could change social categories in life. Not surprisingly, almost every single person we talked to told us that the situation of young people, whether women or men, is generally not good. There is deep unhappiness with the lack of work and the depth of poverty in Burundi, in both rural and urban areas. Equally unsurprisingly, the first answer to the 'what would you do if you were admicom [*administrateur communal* – communal administrator]' question relates to jobs, at least in the city; in the countryside, to assistance. The few exceptions included some rural people who seemed to feel at ease with their prospects, mainly in Nyanza-Lac, as well as some of the urban highest-income group, who seemed to be talking about another country altogether: 'Young people follow the classical path of going to university. Then they get work in public or private sector outfits. Those who fail emigrate to the West.' (This is a quote from a retired army officer.)

A limited number of factors are widely considered the prime drivers of people's economic station in life. High up comes education – unsurprisingly. Parental situation was mentioned often, as well: how wealthy a boy's or a girl's parents are; the values parents instilled in their children; the degree of division that reigns in the family (for example, it is widely understood that children from polygamous marriages fare less well in life because of the divisions in the household). As a nineteen-year-old urban man told us:

> Those who have parents who work, they study. The others don't study: if your parents are too poor and you don't get enough food in the stomach, you cannot study. Some of those who didn't study are lucky enough to have jobs – work on buses, for example. Others have no work at all, so they don't do anything, or get occasional small jobs. Even the children of ministers are afraid their parents will die and they will fall deeply.

For women, marriage was also frequently mentioned as a determinant of well-being. Marriage can bring economic and, especially, social security. This thirty-year-old rural man summed up prevailing wisdom:

> Girls' situation is completely dependent on the men they marry. If they come from a rich family, and marry a poor man, they can become a lot worse off – and vice versa. Unmarried girls either come from rich families and have easy lives, or they come from

poor families. If the parents are dynamic, their situations can improve. When the parents are not dynamic, they stay poor.

But far and away the most popular explanation of people's economic situation falls under the rubric of 'personal character.' This whole area of personal responsibility, success and failure, and social marginalization is at the very heart of how Burundians interpret their society.

Very often, conversations contain references to the *centre de negoce* and the *ligala* and, for women, 'prostitution.' These are the key words to describe people who don't live the way society values – 'deviant' or 'marginal' people, in sociological language. The *centre de negoce* refers to a market area, often very small, where people come to buy and sell things. There is often a slew of little bars there, maybe someone selling goat brochettes, a couple of boutiques and vegetable sellers, and a few artisan shops – bike and shoe repair, maybe. Youth hangs out there, especially in the afternoon. *Ligala* is a Swahili word that simply denotes a place to hang out. It could be any public place where people congregate. It is a word with a negative connotation – as is *centre de negoce*, when used in this way. There is an element of idleness associated with it, of drunkenness, of menace and petty criminality. In Bujumbura, it also has an association with the violent events of the beginning of the war: gangs of youth hanging out at *ligalas* undertook many of the brutal killings during those awful years. 'Prostitution' similarly denotes a fall from grace, a failure to live up to expectations of productivity and chastity by women. All these, then, are images used mainly for young people, and their power lies in their association with failure.

Words describing moralistic or deviant behavior appeared in a whopping 185 conversations – in other words, more than half of all those with whom we spoke about the situation of young people spontaneously talked about prostitution and/or the *ligala*. Especially in the city, this was a constant refrain: it appeared 145 times there (out of approximately 170, meaning that more than 80 percent of all conversations we had in the city included

TABLE 5.3 Discussions, and explanations, of men's marginal behavior

	<30	>30	M	F	Rural	Urban	Total
Poverty	9	8	14	3	10	7	17
Value changes	14	5	15	4	6	13	19
Laziness and other character flaws	29	5	21	12	6	28	34
No explanation	11	6	9	8	4	13	17
TOTAL	63	24	59	27	26	61	87

TABLE 5.4 Discussions, and explanations, of women's marginal behavior

	<30	>30	M	F	Rural	Urban	Total
Poverty	27	7	24	10	3	31	34
Value changes	17	3	11	9	3	17	20
Laziness and other character flaws	18	5	18	5	6	17	23
No explanation	16	5	16	5	2	19	21
TOTAL	78	20	69	29	14	84	98

mention of prostitution and criminality). In the rural areas, the frequency was about one quarter.

But people did not all give the same explanation for these phenomena. In one discourse, the situation of marginal youth was explained by their character weakness. 'Many young men behave well, but some do not. Those young men think they behave in modern, developed ways, but this is dirty behavior, a step back. [...] They are the ones who brought AIDS here' (twenty-three-year-old male farmer, Nyanza-Lac). Or this thirty-year-old bike taxi driver: 'I know young men who are afraid of jobs that demand a lot of effort. It is this category of youth that becomes lazy and transforms itself into bandits when evening comes.

When you work hard you will obtain the necessary for yourself and your family.' Or listen to this twenty-year-old poor returned refugee's judgment about women:

> Most young women are hypocrites. When they finish the morning work, they make themselves beautiful and start to circulate in the streets. I admire those from the neighboring *collines* who are more disciplined and love to cultivate the land. When they have finished the morning work, young men and women often meet at the *ligala* and behave as couples. Then they go to the bars. There are those who listen to the advice of their parents and those who just do what comes up in their heads.

Their responses reflect a very conservative, moralistic interpretation of social reality. We found it everywhere, not just among certain groups: this discourse seems determined not by an objective structural position, but rather by a person's values – their religious values and parental education and personal trajectory.

A very different explanation is what we could call the progressive one (in scholarly terms it would be called 'structural'). In this interpretation, the situation of marginal youth is not the result of their bad behavior, but of the debilitating constraints of poverty, unemployment, and insecurity. 'Everybody here wants to work, the whole city in Bujumbura. They are waiting, even at the *ligala*, but they can't find any work. Young people don't choose to sit down if there is work for them to be had. This also holds for those who are in the *ligala*: it is not laziness, but lack of work that brings them here' (thirty-year-old *ramasseur de bus* – responsible for passenger loading – Musaga). A twenty-four-year-old female farmer who was also *sous-chef de colline* and head of an association describes it thus: 'Young men have nothing to do. They display bad behavior, debauchery, drinking, they don't have jobs and hang out in the streets. The bad behavior is caused by having nothing to do.'

Probably not surprisingly, those whom we interviewed who were themselves marginalized youth often (but by no means always) adhered to this analysis. For example, this is how a twenty-three-year-old refugee explains her life: 'I lived with my paternal grandfather, but he is poor and I had to fend for myself, and that is how I started to frequent men, not because I like it but only to have enough to eat.' This argument is made a lot more frequently about women than about men, often involving the explanation that it is much harder for women to find decent work than for men.

A third position argues that society has changed, values have deteriorated, bad examples abound, cultural pressures weaken morals, and families do not educate their children well anymore. Quite frequently, in this interpretation, international factors are invoked: foreign movies, the presence of *Bazungu*, the UN peacekeeping mission (ONUB). 'Young women don't have good behavior, but it is the behavior of the parents that explains that. If the parents let them often go to the cinema, no wonder their behavior will be marginal' (seventeen-year-old urban IDP). 'Youth here is like in any other city: they only think of having fun. It is the same thing for girls: you see them walking in the street with their telephones, doing nothing' (nineteen-year-old former child soldier).

Burundians, thus, display a wide range of ideological positions on the issue of marginal youth. Essentially, the same sort of political positions that exist in Western societies can be found among ordinary Burundians. They range from conservative to progressive and differ in the degree of individual versus collective responsibility they assign. These opinions seem to cut across location, gender, and economic class. In other words, people's analyses are more than structurally determined: they make choices in terms of their values, their background, their sense of direction, their religion, etc. Note that the presence of this sort of ideological cleavage makes it perfectly possible to envision party politics in Burundi: there is more to the country than ethnic politics.

Our results counter a certain interpretation of gender roles in Africa. On the one hand, they do confirm what has been found elsewhere, namely how labeling can be a potent form of social control. From colonial Uganda and Asante to modern-day Rwanda, researchers have found that women, adjusting to economic pressure by taking on roles traditionally reserved for men, are often labeled as prostitutes, and 'loose women' (Allman 2001: 131–43; Musisi 2001: 181–4; Jefremovas 1991: 379). Such labeling is especially prevalent in countries that have experienced instability or undergone rapid change, as is certainly the case in Burundi (Hodgson and McCurdy 2001: 114; Enloe 2005). Our results differ significantly from this literature, however, in two ways. First, in our conversations, this discourse on character weakness applied more to men than to women. Second, other discourses, regarding both men and women, were also often heard.

Indeed, contrary to much of the literature that treats this sort of discourse as applying only to women – a particular form of gendered stereotyping and, ultimately, symbolic gendered violence – it is to *men* that it is more frequently applied. By far the most prevalent approach to marginal men is the moralistic, conservative one. In my recollection, many of the harshest judges of young men are other young men, often migrants who have come to the city in recent years fleeing rural misery and unemployment. They work very hard, barely scraping by, sending money to their families, saving to build a house at home or to improve their business. Their negative judgment is of those – often urban born – who they believe let themselves go, flee into drinking and drugs, and generally don't try hard enough.

The progressive explanation is far more prevalent for women than for men. Men's 'deviant' behavior is explained by poverty by 24 percent of the people we spoke to, whereas for women this figure is 44 percent. Clearly, people generally are more understanding of the fate of women: they had less choice, people are telling me – their lives are harder. This assessment prevails among both women and men – but in our interviews it is actually among *men* that this interpretation is more prevalent. This is interesting, for these same people live lives in which traditional gender roles still dominate. It is as if they are looking in from the outside, knowing and analyzing what happens to women – but still maintaining the traditional roles.

Our discussions of mobility shed more light on this. Frequently, after the previous question about the situation of young men/women, we added a follow-up question, namely: 'Is it possible for people to change categories?' This was our way of probing into people's analysis of social mobility. Frankly, I expected that the large majority of people would answer me negatively, telling me that the rich stay rich and the poor stay poor. To my great surprise, we heard many more affirmative answers than negative ones: the majority of Burundian youth told me that social mobility *is* possible, and they had arguments and examples about how it can be done. Note that most of them were clear that it was not a frequent occurrence, and that downward social mobility is more likely than upward social mobility. Nevertheless, this deep sense of potential mobility surprised me. The key factors involved are hard work and perseverance, good management, and dynamism. Just hear their voices.

Hard work and perseverance

There is social mobility. All families in this camp lost everything, including their house, when they came here. Some were discouraged, had no hope to continue living, let go. They became indigent. Others, notwithstanding theft and despair, started again, looked for opportunities and improved their situation very much. (Eighteen-year-old female student, Ruhororo)

I know young men who work during the day in security and study at night. Other young men manage to improve their businesses. I know a young man who began by selling three pants and now he has so many he can't put them on his shoulder anymore and had to get a stand at the market to sell them. His business is bigger than 200,000 francs now. Others, by bad luck or bad management, don't manage to progress or even fall into bankruptcy. (Twenty-nine-year-old poor migrant worker, Musaga)

At some point, we asked people what would happen if they were unable to achieve their goals. Most of our interviewees displayed an astounding amount of perseverance and tenacity.

Many people sounded more fatalistic – whatever befell them was part of God's larger plan – but even then, there was a deep undercurrent of perseverance. Here are some examples:

> In all cases I'd continue to seek for whatever may be possible. I will not give up without having enough to feed my children. (Twenty-three-year-old female IDP in the lowest economic category, Musaga)

> After the war, there are those dynamic ones who have started to improve the situation. Others, however, have sold everything they had because they became discouraged. (Twenty-nine-year-old female farmer, Ruhororo)

> I know a young man who started selling peanuts and who now owns a well-filled boutique, with a value of 300,000 francs. I also know a girl who started selling little things and now bought a piece of land for a value of 300,000 francs. To get there, you need a lot of work and luck because there are many who fail after a certain time. (Twenty-year-old man sewing clothes, Musaga)

> After all I have lived through, it would be stupid of me to despair. One must always maintain hope. It has happened to me that I wanted to end my life, but the next day I regretted having thought that. These are moments that you tell yourself it is worthwhile to persevere. (Twenty-three-year-old female refugee in the lowest economic category, Bwiza)

Perseverance is so important to these young people. Most of these quotes are from the poorest of the poor. They know that life is hard, that failure is likely, but they also intend never to give up. In the literature on young men in Africa, it has become so common to describe them only as angry, frustrated, drifting into mindless violence – potential rapists and killers, all of them, it seems. In some theories, their very existence is taken as an indicator of violence, regardless of their personalities, beliefs, dreams. And yet, when you talk with them, how different they are from these simplistic images – how filled with perseverance and hope, ready to take on life and all that it may bring.

These lines should also once and for all lay to rest the constant repetition of the dependency syndrome argument in development circles. How many hundreds of times have I heard that argument – the poor depend on our aid; helping the poor is dangerous – expressed by high-earning intellectuals, local and foreign. Aid dependency, it seems, acts as an explanation for every negative social phenomenon. It is also condescending nonsense, spouted by people who would not survive for a week the life conditions of those they talk about.

Good management and responsibility

Men who are in a good situation can fall into bankruptcy if they hang out with girls with bad behaviors. They start to spend more than they earn and find themselves without money. When a girl starts a business, she thinks only of her business. It happens rarely that she goes bankrupt. The big problem for girls is to accumulate enough funds to have a start-up capital. (Thirty-year-old male waiter in a bar in Musaga)

It happens that young people manage to improve their level, especially when they have a business that works well and they limit their expenses to the absolute minimum. It happens that someone who sells peanuts becomes a seller in a small ambulant store. Me, I know that I will finish by quitting this job to become a seller of dried fish. There are those who fall because they waste their money or are careless and lose it all or are fired by their bosses. For girls, the risk of falling is bigger because the products they sell at the market are very perishable. Others become pregnant and aren't capable of working anymore. (Twenty-three-year-old male seller of phone cards, Kamenge)

Dynamism

Some young men I know have become rich because of their dynamism. Some of them even came from poor families. They may have started selling peanuts in little plastic bags and now they are big traders. (Twenty-six-year-old farmer who also had animals and a little trade on the side) [talking about his hopes for his children] They will be dynamic in life and become good managers. I don't expect them to study because I don't have enough money to pay for that. In that respect, they will have to endure the life of their father. But everything depends on their personality, because every bit of money that they earn, even at a young age, they can use to start a small business. I know big traders who started by selling peanuts. (Twenty-eight-year-old farmer, no formal education at all)

I admire every young person who doesn't let destiny decide for him. Destiny will find you if you remain sitting down. I advise youth to stop with the bad habit of staying all day in the *ligala*, and to get working to evolve in life. (Twenty-two-year-old poor farmer, returned from displacement camp)

Illegal means

In many conversations, people also made the observation that illegal or extralegal means may also sustain economic mobility, whether upward or downward. Here, too, they sometimes had examples. Politics, theft, and the war came up frequently here.

Some people gained during the war through dishonest means. They don't greet you or talk to you anymore because you know too much about them. (Fifty-five-year-old widow in Ruhororo; gets assent from three to four other people her age)

A trader can become rich too. I know one who started selling petrol in little cans for fifty francs, and now he has a whole fleet of trucks and buildings and more than ten employees. [Did he do that cleanly?] You are right: a lot of theft and clientelism goes on. During the crisis, for example, much was stolen and sold cheaply at the bazaar, where others bought it for nothing and made a lot of money later. Other businessmen had close relations to the army or the rebels and benefited when their turn came. Fraud and corruption is the fastest way to get rich. If you are honest you will not earn much. (Twenty-four-year-old university student, Bujumbura)

Young men live very badly because of the crisis. They are under-employed, but there are others who have profited from the crisis by stealing and pillaging. Some, thus, have made strides during the crisis and others fell down. They consequently live very differently. (Thirty-seven-year-old urban teacher, university education)

Here we touch at the underbelly of mobility. Hard work, perseverance, dynamism – all well and good, but political connections, sexual favors, corruption, or theft can bring people much farther much faster – and everyone knows it.

When intellectuals told me about anger in Burundian society, they often talked about houses as well – how ordinary people see villas being built whereas they still live in run-down shacks. There is an interesting point here: the popular anger is often more from the winning side, the one in power, for it is there that disappointment is the biggest; it is there that the fate of leaders and followers most visibly diverges, with the former making it big-time and the latter often finding their lives unchanged (Pouligny 2006: 59). This is why the anger in Kamenge, a radical Hutu neighborhood par excellence, is so much greater and more palpable than in Musaga, a Tutsi neighborhood that is hardly better off.

Help, self-help, mutual help

Following a discussion of people's plans or projects for the future, we asked: 'Who helps you with your plan?' It is to the analysis of these answers we now turn.

As can be seen in Table 5.5, by far the biggest category of answers consists of negative ones. Only in Busiga and Nyanza-Lac did international aid agencies get mentioned with any frequency. These were primarily humanitarian INGO programs: CARE, which had built houses for IDPs in Ruhororo, and distributed goats, food, and water points throughout the province; NRC and ADRA in Nyanza-Lac for their support to returning refugees and IDPs.

Very striking as well is the almost total disappearance of

TABLE 5.5 Answers to the 'who helps you' question, by area

	Busiga	Ruhororo	Nyanza-Lac	Musaga	Kamenge	Bwiza	Other urban	Total
Nobody/no agencies ever helped	21	17	24	42	17	5	8	134
Family	10	5	17	13	19	9	10	83
International NGOs[1]	31	9	26	0	0	0	0	66
National NGOs[2]	7	0	0	5	10[4]	3	1	26
Bank/Credit Union	0	1	2	0	0	3	12	18
International organization[5]	3	0	1	0	5	1	2	12
National human rights NGOs[3]	0	1	1	1	0	0	0	3
TOTAL	72	33	71	61	51	21	33	

Notes: 1. Mainly CARE in Ngozi and ADRA and CNR in Nyanza-Lac. 2. References were to SWAA, THARS, CARITAS, and Centre Jeunes Kamenge. 3. One mention of Ligue Iteka for getting land back on which a displacement camp is built (no success); one of APRODH for a person unjustly accused and imprisoned (successful), and one of Association des Femmes Juristes for support after a rape (ongoing). 4. Seven out of ten were references to Centre Jeunes Kamenge, which is without doubt the most recognized organization I met in Burundi during six months of research. 5. Mentions of WFP, UNICEF, HCR.

international aid in the city of Bujumbura. Not a single person out of more than 150 with whom we discussed this in Bujumbura mentioned an international NGO,[6] and only a handful mentioned a multilateral agency (mainly UNICEF for school books). This says something about a very odd phenomenon, namely the almost total neglect of the city by the international development community. If one takes away the 1 square mile where the ministries are and where the foreigners and senior civil servants live, the international community has no presence in Bujumbura. Apart from the jobs it creates for the fortunate few, the international community's impact is chiefly felt by the price hikes for rent and food, which have repercussions all the way down the line, and the big white SUVs passing by at high speed with their mysterious occupants behind tinted glass.

There exists a traditional donor perception, backed up by government rhetoric, that poverty is rural only. This view is mistaken for two important reasons. First, there is a lot of poverty in the city. Second, the city is deeply connected to the countryside: not only does it offer a place for young men to escape rural stagnation, but these people invest much of what they earn in the city back in the countryside. This urban neglect is dangerous too, for it is in the city that the conditions for violence are by far the most ripe: the dense concentration of ex-combatants, the deep frustration felt by many as a result of their relative impoverishment and the visibility of the wealth of the new elite, and the presence of counter-elites with deep pockets willing to buy themselves some shock troops.

Burundians overwhelmingly presented a picture of being without support, of facing life's difficulties alone, of not being able to count on much except their families and friends. The table above doesn't really capture well the tenor of our conversations: the high figures for some agencies make it look as if there was general appreciation of support received, but such is certainly not the case: most of these answers came grudgingly, were said in a way that suggested the smallness of the aid received, or were accompanied by references to corruption.

Of the local institutions in Burundi – the ones not dependent on or inspired by international aid – the only one that is mentioned frequently is the family. This is logical: it is from here that the funds come which allow families to invest in what matters to them. Recent data show, for example, that educational expenses are paid for 66 percent by fathers, 15 percent by mothers, 2.8 percent by the government, 1 percent by the children themselves, and 0.8 percent by aid agencies (MINIPLAN 2006: 57) – so much for aid dependence.

Mutual help At the same time as the family was mentioned as the prime source of aid for people's projects, people talked to us, over and over, about the decline in social solidarity. This argument came in two versions: one stresses that mutual help has gone down because there is no more love between people, and another that social relations between the rich and the poor are getting worse and worse. A quote from an old widow in Ruhororo camp brings these both together. Her life story was very sad, and she was clearly angry at the way life had treated her: her whole body moved as she told stories of how her children and husband died, her land was stolen, her sons left, their whereabouts unknown to her, aid never reaches her. At the same time, she was so poised, so forceful, and she had asked us to talk to her.

> At one point, I was sick. I was in a coma, and had to be brought to the hospital, where I got a transfusion. When I had to pay, I did not have the money and was forced to sell part of my land to a neighbor. In the past, my neighbors would have lent money, but now I have to sell my land. Now I die before his eyes, but it doesn't matter to him. Mutual help has declined, people don't love each other anymore. Before, neighbors would help each other, but not anymore. Now the poor only have social relations with the poor and the rich with the rich.

We heard a very similar story in Nyanza-Lac, from a young repatriated farmer this time.

Recently I have known difficulties and nobody came to my help. My wife was poisoned and even my mother did nothing to help. One of my friends then proposed to buy everything I have and I accepted to save my wife and she became better. But if he had been a better friend he would have lent me the money.

There were significant regional variations. The majority of the people who bemoaned the loss of mutual help and social solidarity came from Ruhororo. Indeed, as many as 80 percent of the remarks on this subject in rural areas came from this commune, *and they came from both the IDP camp and the remote* colline. This suggests that the social malaise in Ruhororo is felt equally strongly among the displaced people (a small Tutsi ghetto) and those who are at home (primarily Hutu).

Of course, we encountered instances of solidarity as well, even in Ruhororo: while we were talking with the old widow there, an old man began putting a new straw roof on her house. In Banda *colline*, we talked to three young men, aged nineteen, twenty and twenty-two, who were building a house for the oldest one. The middle one gave us the standard mutual help line: he was helping his friend to build a house and believed his friend would return the favor some day when he needed it. But then the younger one added, with typical honesty and the insight of youth:

> Also, we should not hide the truth that one chooses one's friends according to their economic level. If, for example, we had a friend who is very poor and is not envisioning to build a house soon, he would say that he is wasting his time with mutual help, because we would not be able to return the service to him. So we'd have to pay him.

And in the same town, another young man told us something very similar.

> If a young man is from a rich family, he gets a lot of help from those who are at the same level and who can receive something in return. Who could provide service to someone who can't return the favor? Social relations are like this: rich to rich, poor to poor.

113

By all accounts, mutual help – carrying a sick person to the hospital, feeding a hungry neighbor, preparing the land of a person too old to do it – was the default mode in the countryside until recently. Many people told us it had disappeared because of the war. Two mechanisms may have caused this: the divisions that emerged within communities, and the dramatic impoverishment of people. The fact that in better-off Nyanza-Lac people bemoaned the decline in mutual help significantly less suggests that it is primarily the economic-crisis impact of the war which is important.

Some people explained the decline in mutual help by the spread of new values – the move from a moral economy to a capitalist one, so to speak. A young migrant student in Bujumbura explained this argument well to me:

> here, while learning the languages at school you also learn the cultural assumptions that are built into it, and they are of individualism and consumption. You take this over. You know, Peter, now, when someone from my family in the interior comes by, I barely give them five minutes; when someone is dying along the road, I look the other way.

This sort of long-term cultural-change explanation, resulting from the spread of market relations and education, is an old argument, and I frequently heard it when I worked in the Burundian countryside two decades ago. It has an immediate, anthropological type of appeal, but I am not sure it is correct. First, money (and taxes) were introduced in Burundi many decades ago now, but people see the decline in mutual help as a much more recent phenomenon – as witnessed by the instances they recall of past mutual help. Second, it does not seem that mutual help is much less prevalent in the urban world, as it should be if market relations and cultural individualism were the prime driving forces. Surprisingly, many more urban than rural interviewees spontaneously said that mutual help is alive and well in the neighborhoods they live in, and they gave me many examples.

My sister and I assure the needs of our mother, who doesn't work anymore, as well as the wife and child of my older brother, who recently died of sickness. Here, notwithstanding the few means and the daily difficulties, there is a lot of love and mutual solidarity. I could not go home to eat now, for example, without telling my friends that the one who is hungry can come with me. If I do not have enough they will see it and voluntarily tell me, 'No thanks, it is just enough for you.' (Twenty-five-year-old driver, born in the city)

Yes, there is mutual help, for we all are in the same situation. If I have no salt today, I can go to my neighbor and ask. And tomorrow he can ask me for salt. If I have nothing to eat, the same thing. (Twenty-five-year-old woman, street seller)

The fact that urban youths, a rather alienated and unhappy bunch to begin with, living in conditions of squalor, very often far removed from their nuclear families, systematically assure me that mutual help is alive and well in their neighborhood is telling. At the very least, even if it is not entirely factually true, it means that there is still a positive premium placed on mutual help, which may explain why people seek to convince me of its existence, or why they overestimate its presence. But I believe it is also possible that their words describe a real-life phenomenon. In the city, there is no family that does not have people from the larger family, or from the native commune, living in its house;[7] there is no weekend that passes without envelopes of money being handed out for celebrations, for education, and for a never-ending list of needs and obligations.

That said, *all* urban people did recognize problems with mutual help as well, and they invoked the most prosaic reason for it: the dramatic poverty that characterizes people's lives. What they told me, in other words, is that a norm in favor of mutual help still exists, but it is constantly challenged by the fact that people have as good as nothing.

[so, there is mutual help here?] Yes, but not much. It is because the others have very little too. They have many kids and must feed them too, so if you arrive too late, the plate is empty. It is not by badness or lack of trust: it is by poverty. (Twenty-four-year-old unemployed man)

Mutual aid does exist. If we survive, it's because of that. It changed, though. There used to be peace and people loved each other. If you asked for something, you could not be refused. Now you'll only be given if you can give too, for it is hard to find things to eat. If people give you something, they won't find something else to replace it with. [...] Someone of high standing passes in a car, and will not notice you on foot. The place he lives in, you can't get to. His places to drink and relax in you can't afford. (Nineteen-year-old unemployed man)

One of the striking images I carry with me from this research into life in Burundi is the degree of segmentation in society: how economic groups live physically close to each other but with little exchange. This very much undermines the notion of community as a bounded geographical entity. In the development business, we have been told for years that 'community' participation may hide significant differences in wealth and power. Certainly this is strongly reinforced by the results of our conversations, which clearly suggest that, even in what look like traditional, poor, and closely bounded spaces, there exists major and structural segmentation; as a result, individuals – the 'youth leader' or the 'women's representative' – may really only speak for themselves or offer the perspective on life of their own income group.

Conclusion: Burundi is a capitalist paradise

All Burundians we spoke to told us they have been materially hurt by the war. The litany of theft and destruction, of forced migration, of education years lost, and of family members and friends killed, is unending. Almost nobody, it seems, whether rural or urban, rich or poor, has not seen their meager assets depleted if not eradicated entirely by the war.

At the same time, the war is not the full story of people's

economic evolution over the years. Rural people, especially in the north, consider that population growth and what they term climate change have been equally important – and problematic – in affecting their lives. The war may have captured all the attention, but many other economic and ecological dynamics continue unabated.

A surprising proportion of people told us they lived better lives than their parents – even after twelve years of war. Some of this was about modernization – women's empowerment, surely a growing reality in Burundi (see the next chapter), or more general economic diversification. A lot of it was about migration – people escaping the prison of agriculture, trying different things, having a sense of possibility, no matter how small. In most countries, war provokes urban migration, and Burundi seems to be no exception. This urbanization is considered a step forward by many young people (not all: I recall some women, for example, whose forced migration to the city was catastrophic, depriving them of support and leaving them vulnerable to sexual predation), and may have positive impacts on the rural areas where these people come from, as they send money back to their parents.

Few make it in the city – as in the countryside. But some do, and everyone knows of such people. Those who manage to improve their fate are widely admired – all the more if they did so legally. Burundians are deep believers in the most Weberian values of hard work, perseverance, savings, and good management.

To conclude, let me try to synthesize the story of development as seen by Burundian youth. Individual effort is at the heart of young Burundians' station in life. It is through intelligence and studying, through hard work, perseverance and good management, that they hope to improve their fate. They expect little to nothing of the state or of the aid system. Family members continue to be the main source of support, although there is a significant decline in their ability and willingness to provide mutual aid.

What is it young people try to do when they work hard to

117

escape poverty? In the northern rural areas, diversification *out of agriculture* is absolutely crucial. Education is the main way of achieving this, but there is also a very strong demand for vocational training. Migration is also crucial for many poor young men – but probably not the poorest, who need it most. While there remains widespread social resistance against migration too, especially for young women, it is a recognized fact of life.

In the city, young men and women want only three things: jobs, jobs, and jobs. Only a lucky few have truly good jobs, like those in NGOs or the United Nations – the ones you need education and good social connections for. The overwhelming majority of the others live in the informal sector, selling products along the road, working in bars, in houses, doing little bits of artisanry or heavy lifting. Many of these jobs are temporary and earn extremely little. Those who manage to save money – to build a house and marry; to invest in a better business – do so through constant sacrifice and stunning self-control. They survive by drawing on the values of frugality, forward thinking, and resilience. A sense of destiny and the support of God are important in this.

People often present harsh judgments of those at the margin, especially urban young men. They are regarded as having failed to live by the values of perseverance, hard work, and resilience that Burundians value. Many people fear them. A negative atti-tude to idle youth, then, is widespread, not only among the elites but also among ordinary people. But not all people are harsh. Some do not judge marginalized youth on the basis of their personal attributions, but rather ascribe their misery to structural factors – poverty and violence. This more 'progressive' analysis is especially prevalent in the case of marginal young women: there is a widely shared opinion that young women who engage in prostitution do so through force and need, and not through character weakness. In short, there are clear ideological differ-ences between Burundians; they don't all think alike, and they sure don't all think the way aid agencies tend to.

Aid seems to hardly relate to these dynamics. Because people see life improvement as individual – the result of personal choices

118

and hard work – collective development actions are not popular. Credit (individual, preferably) is very important, as can be insurance and protection against shocks, especially of sickness. But at its core, job creation is the only key to development. Nothing else matters. Any way to promote job creation must be pursued: decentralized vocational training that builds on local economic dynamics and resources; the transformation of primary products; economic networks that bring to the growing cities the food, artisanal, and other products they need; intermediate technologies that use local resources, including in the field of recycling and trash removal; public works that create employment during low economic periods at the same time as maintaining infrastructure; training in basic business skills for young men and women, as well as simplified and preferably non-corrupt procedures for establishing small businesses. A productivist – as opposed to welfarist – approach to development is what Burundians themselves talk about. Burundi truly is a capitalist paradise, at least as far as its citizens' attitudes are concerned.

This capitalist ethos has long roots in Burundi. The way people describe it, Burundian society used to be a tight and complicated balance between individual initiative and communal obligation. Individual success was always appreciated and encouraged. What a man earned belonged to him and nobody else, and someone who earned more was admired for that. As a young migrant worker in Nyanza-Lac told me: 'in our region, a son who becomes better off than his father will become a *mushingantahe* before him.' At the same time, there was a strong expectation of mutual help: if you had food or tools, you would share this with your neighbors. If you failed to live up to this code, the social pressure could be great indeed, but it was your personal decision, as the individual owner – there was no organized redistributive mechanism.

The modern combination of individualism and mutual aid, then, builds on long-term historical dynamics. On the other hand, there is a rupture here. A decline in mutual help is occurring. Structural changes of growing destitution, population growth, pervasive violence, and the systematic uprooting of communities have made life far harder than it ever used to be. The war is at the heart of many of these negative trends, but it is by no means the only factor. People also see – and discuss – how social and political connections, corruption and outright criminality allow some individuals to advance greatly, and make others lose. Burundians typically do not develop a structural analysis of their society: they observe empirical differences in how some won and some lost and they are angry about corruption and politicians, but they do not make a class analysis. They look at life in a far more individualistic manner (reflecting the way they regard human rights and citizenship).

By calling it a capitalist ethos, I make it sound wholly positive and desirable, especially to Americans, who have been told that there is no more beautiful way of organizing life than unbridled capitalism and individual competition. But the spread of this cut-throat capitalism constitutes a profound loss for Burundi as well. Burundi's capitalist ethos feeds on fear and desperation – the knowledge that destitution and death lurk around every corner, that nobody is there to help you, and that you can only count on your own actions to survive, day by day, month by month.

In a country where people are with their backs against the wall, and where there is no rule of law, the sort of capitalism that emerges is often a brutal one. It is often a capitalism of unequal power and cheating, where employers cheat their employees, sellers their buyers, and neighbors their neighbors. It is a capitalism where intimidation, political connections, and cunning pervade too many transactions. Burundians bemoan this brutality of life and spend enormous amounts of time and resources protecting themselves against likely cheating and depredation, thus holding back individual incomes as well as macroeconomic growth.

And what is the impact of development aid on all this? On the positive side, development aid, at the end of the war, has invested enormously in promoting primary education. This is as much due to a fine political sense that the new government ought to be supported in a key programmatic goal as to the fact that this particular goal is in any case part of the sacrosanct Millennium Development Goals. Vocational training, crucial to the many people who are forced to leave school, is much more neglected. And some projects work well. In Ngozi province, for example, CARE did nice work with credit for women, in a combined livelihood and gender approach. The DDR program was in the process of providing reinsertion funds to thousands of child and adult ex-combatants.

All of this is worthwhile and important. It leaves enormous gaps as well. The most important of these gaps is the surprising neglect of the urban slums. Especially from a conflict perspective, one imagines that tens of thousands of underemployed urban youth – many of them with first-hand experience of violence – would constitute a major priority, but nothing could be farther from reality. The reasons for this neglect are both political (the government seems to see its power base in the countryside, which is a priori a welcome reversal of decades of Burundian politics) and due to donor misperception of poverty as rural. Be that as it may, young men and women in the city and in the countryside overwhelmingly desire just one thing: to have a steady job. Another important neglected group consists of IDPs, overwhelmingly Tutsi, in the north: they, too, are clearly no political priority to the current government, and the donors seem to have no idea what to do with them either, so they just wither away, neglected by all.

More generally, much aid seems not to be in touch with the productivist, capitalist, individualist ethos of most Burundians. Most aid programming is focused on welfare and community. More reflection is required on how to better match aid modalities and objectives to the life conditions and values of Burundians: this will make it more effective.

There is long-running debate about horizontal inequalities, and how aid ought to decrease those (Stewart 2000; Boyce 2004). This concern did not appear at all in the conversations we had in Burundi. People did not refer to other ethnic groups' economic advantages. Also, not one of our 386 conversations mentioned a problem with the benefits received by ex-combatants, and the sixty-three ex-combatants themselves did not relate to us instances of anger about their advantages either. What did come up in many conversations, however, was both a generic set of complaints about corruption – mainly related to local authorities, but some also spoke about national leaders – and a general disdain of politicians: their luxurious houses in posh neighborhoods were always mentioned. Given that Burundi is historically a country with extremely significant horizontal inequality, these results are interesting. Burundians clearly see the war – and the challenges of the post-war period – as a problem of personal corruption and venal political class, but this is not an ethnic matter (and thus not one of horizontal inequality either) – it is a matter of evil people. Also, lest we forget: these corrupt authorities, at both the local and the national level, are as often Hutu (especially in the post-war situation) as Tutsi.

6 | 'I want to marry a dynamic girl': changing gender expectations in Burundi[1]

KIM HOWE AND PETER UVIN

This chapter analyzes norms and practices of masculinity and femininity in Burundi. We asked people, old and young, men and women, what expectations they hold of their boys and their girls, or what expectations their parents had of them. We asked people what is a man, what is an adult, whom they respect, and why. We asked others whom they wanted to marry – that always made them laugh, but also provided us with further insight into masculine and feminine ideals. In addition, we constantly gendered most of our other interview questions. Whether discussing the situation of youth, migration, or plans for the future, we asked interviewees to address how their responses would be different for men than for women. We thus have three sources of information about gender in Burundi: first, the answers to explicit questions about gender roles; second, the comparison of answers given by men and by women to all our interview questions; and, third, the way interviewees themselves differentiated the situation of men from that of women.

In much of sub-Saharan Africa and the rest of the world, the main requirement to become 'a man' is to marry and provide for a family. Marriage requires bride wealth as well as money for the construction of a house and the organization of the festivities. Historically, these costs were borne by the father of the groom, but increasingly families are not capable of maintaining this tradition. The responsibility for covering the full costs of marriage thus falls to the young men themselves, but without jobs, income, or land, this proves extremely difficult for them as well (Correia and Bannon 2006: 245). As a result, in much of sub-Saharan Africa the average marriage age has risen, and desirable young women are picked as second or third wives – or as concubines – by better-off older men. And even those men who manage to marry may not be able to provide for their families.

Throughout Africa, then, men fail to reach normative 'manhood,' and as a result suffer profound personal frustration and social embarrassment. This often leads to alcoholism, low self-esteem and depression, multi-partnered sexual relationships (with clear implications for the spread of HIV/AIDS), violence against women, and, at worst, participation in violent political conflict (Silberschmidt 2001: 657; Barker and Ricardo 2006: 161–77; Sommers 2007: 153; Hyden 2006: 153, 165; Amuyunzu-Nyamongo and Francis 2006: 220, 223). Richards (2006) has argued that this is one of the root causes of young men's involvement in the civil war in Sierra Leone. Does this argument also hold for Burundi?

The primary role ascribed to women in sub-Saharan Africa is to marry, have children, and take care of the household. Women are responsible for the subsistence of their families and for producing children to secure additional labor (Hyden 2006: 165, 167). Even educated women are supposed to meet traditional obligations of marriage, childbearing, and domestic work (Sall 2000: xv; Kwesiga 2002: 139). In general terms, women's proscribed behavior is couched in moralistic terms and includes obedience, deference to men, and sexual chastity (Jefremovas 1991: 379, 383). Women who do not conform to these ideals are often labeled as 'immoral,' 'wicked,' or 'prostitutes.' They are embarrassments to their families and ostracized by their communities (Hodgson and McCurdy 2001: 1). Is this the case for Burundi as well? And has the war changed anything in this respect? These are the sorts of broader questions that guided us.

Marriage

One of the most significant mechanisms through which gender ideology is produced and reproduced is marriage (Silberschmidt 2001: 659). In Africa, marriage is a cornerstone in the attainment of 'manhood' and 'womanhood'; it gives one a social identity and is a crucial part of achieving adulthood (Kwesiga 2002: 58).

Spinsters are generally not respected in African communities and they are an embarrassment to the family. Bachelors do not command the same social respect that married men do (Okeke 2001: 239; Kwesiga 2002: 139).

Our interviews with rural Burundians largely confirm the notion that marriage is a hallmark in the achievement of 'manhood' and 'womanhood.' When asked a general question about their plans for the future, 58 of the 117 young unmarried men we interviewed spontaneously told us they wanted to marry or build a house – almost always an indication of a plan to marry. Plans focusing on marriage were higher in the countryside than in the city, but still a good number of young urban men, especially migrants, described marriage as their main plan for the future.

Historically in Burundi, young women marry in their late teens, and young men slightly later. The family of the groom makes sure the new couple has a house to live in and land to cultivate; they will also pay for the dowry (crucial, for without dowry the new father has no rights over his children; Trouwborst 1962: 136ff.) and the ceremony. For the first two years or so after the marriage, the family of the groom supports the new couple in various ways, including by preparing their meals. This ends with a ceremony in which the young family becomes fully independent. At this point, the husband acquires full financial and social responsibility for his wife and children.

In our conversations, the overwhelming majority of people told us that young men face difficulties meeting marriage expectations because they lack land and/or the financial resources necessary to accumulate the requisite bride wealth and support their future wives and children. Only well-off households still manage to support their children's marriage – and thus, in rural areas, when one meets people who are married at a young age, they are typically the better off.

> Most young men desire to marry, but can't because of poverty. They can't build a house, or even buy pants or shoes. Some have parents who help – they build the house and pay bride wealth –

and they are the ones who can get married. (Twenty-five-year-old woman from the IDP camp)

I will only marry if I am economically secure. The age of marriage is getting higher, for young men need to save. In the past, parents financed the wedding, such as the bride wealth, they also paid for the house and celebration, but now there is too much poverty. (Twenty-year-old man, Busiga)

My parents grew up in a time of economic and political stability and as a result had few problems. For example, as they were well off, no boy could achieve my age and still be unmarried. The father would do all that is needed to marry him, but nowadays the boy must help himself in everything that is required to marry. (Twenty-five-year-old man, Nyanza-Lac)

A number of poor young men – the young IDPs in Ruhororo camp, doing nothing all day and without hope for a better future; the self-demobilized, feeling that their sacrifices are totally neglected and without impact on their lives; and orphans, cut off from their families and without access to land – told us that they would *never* marry – a sure sign of their sense of despair and social exclusion. This was talked about with great frustration, defeat, and shame. Listen to the words of this twenty-nine-year-old from Ruhororo when we asked him whom he wanted to marry:

I could never list the qualities of my future spouse if I don't have the slightest plan for marriage. Who would accept to come and live with me in my misery? But the woman I would like to have would be dynamic and would accept to try and earn her living working for others like I do. On top of it, I'd love it if she would respect me notwithstanding my poverty.

Young men seek, of course, to respond to the tough situation they are in. We have already documented that urban migration is a widespread and at least partially successful answer to the challenges of marriage faced by young men. Many of those we met in the city told us they had come to earn sufficient money to be able to marry, they were building a house in their region of origin, or they had already married and returned here to earn further money for the survival of their households.

Another prevalent strategy for managing the hardships of traditional marriage is to engage in 'unofficial' or illegal marriages, also called 'cohabitation' or 'informal union' in the literature. While this is illegal in Burundi, many interviewees described how they and others around them are doing it. All interviewees who talked about unofficial marriage linked it to poverty and the inability of men to come up with marriage-related expenses.

> Young men proceed with illegal cohabitation to avoid the festivity expenditures. Since I returned, there have not been many who have had ceremonies – less than ten – but many have married illegally. (Returned male refugee living in a remote part of Ruhororo)

> In previous times, authorities prohibited it, but now it is difficult to do because a lot of young men must do it because of poverty. How could one imprison them? It is difficult because today few marry legally. (Thirty-three-year-old man in Ruhororo IDP camp)

> Those who are rich do other activities outside of agriculture like animal husbandry and commerce. The majority of them are officially married. The poor live entirely on agriculture, and are not able to have enough means to have an official marriage so they cohabitate illegally. (Thirty-three-year-old demobilized soldier, Busiga)

> Sometimes young men engage in illicit marriage. In principle, all marriage should be legal but it is hard to make this happen. The youth say they are just borrowing the woman until they are ready to buy her. (Fifty-one-year-old returned IDP farmer, Nyanza-Lac)

A trend toward greater cohabitation has also been identified in other parts in Africa, from urban Mozambique to rural Kenya (Amuyunzu-Nyamongo and Francis 2006: 226; Agadjanian 2002). Cohabitation is still seen as less desirable than legal marriage, but what is interesting is that Burundian society seems to consider it understandable and excusable: we heard far fewer condemnations of the practice than a few decades ago; it was usually described as an understandable solution to a tough problem. Some talked of it as an intermediary step to an official marriage – with couples living together for some years while saving for the legal marriage.[2] During this period, the young man might still seek permission from his 'bride's' father to marry, and eventually follow the appropriate steps to a legal marriage (bride wealth, ceremony). In the meantime, however, the couple will likely have children, and the young man will still have financial responsibility for his partner. As a result, some other young men told us that they do not see unofficial marriage as a solution to financial stress.

It is important to observe that while the normalization of informal marriage contributes to social stability, the cost of it is largely borne by women. Indeed, such arrangements put her at risk – if she is thrown out or if he leaves, she is left without legal recourse and often with children, and not welcomed back by her parents. Especially in the city, we met many women who were in that situation, and they were often very badly off.

It is impossible for us to say how frequent this is: how many people who informally marry stay together forever in this informal manner? How many eventually regularize their marriage? One of my drivers did so after twenty-two years of living together and four children, so it is always possible. How many informal marriages dissolve? How many break up, but are renewed after some time? We came across many men for whom the dream of marrying persisted. This unemployed self-demobilized ex-combatant from Kamenge is typical: 'if my situation improved I could go and live with my son and his mother: I would like that, if she is still available.' This wish reflects a value deeply embedded in Burundian culture: fathers should do everything possible to support and raise their children, even those born outside marriage.

Adaptation to hardship: young men and the age of marriage An overwhelming majority of interviewees indicated that the age at which young men are marrying is rising as a result of poverty. These results are identical to those observed in other parts of sub-Saharan Africa (Barker and Ricardo 2006: 156; Richards 2006: 203). In Ngozi province, the poorest rural area we worked in, there was near consensus that the age of marriage for young men is rising.

> Some young men my age are married, but those are the very rich ones. Others do get married, but this is very difficult. If you don't have enough food to feed yourself, it is very difficult to feed a second mouth. I have learned not to marry early – I want sufficient economic basis first. My parents disagree and want me to marry, but I refuse, I want to wait. (Seventeen-year-old male, from a higher economic category, Busiga)

> The marriage age is increasing. I am at the age to get married, but I will only do it in two or three years because I need to save to prepare the marriage and to ensure the life of myself and my children. For those who are not capable of that, they even have to wait beyond twenty-five years old, or abandon their plans entirely. (Nineteen-year-old male, Ruhororo)

While there was a general sense that young men who are able to marry closer to the traditional age (loosely defined as nineteen to twenty-one for young men) are more highly regarded, delays in marriage are considered understandable. This twenty-one-year-old man in the IDP camp spoke about the continued tension between traditional expectations and changing norms: 'Men who stay unmarried long are partly looked upon badly by society. But on the other hand, it is understood because of the great cost.' But significant regional variation exists. In Nyanza-Lac, for example, young men are able to marry at a traditional (younger) age because of their access to productive land and trade opportunities.

> The marriage age has not at all increased here because our region is hot and consequently young people marry early. Many young men manage to earn money early and do not wait long

to marry. We imitate, in fact, the model of our parents. (Twenty-seven-year-old male IDP)

In principle girls marry at eighteen and boys at twenty-one. But here it is a hot region, and one can even marry before that age [he did at twenty]. Of course, it is all a matter of free choice and some marry later, but in general one cannot be older than twenty-five without being married. (Thirty-three-year-old refugee)

Although there was nearly unanimous agreement that the marriage age is rising for men in much of the country, there was less of a consensus about young women. Invoking different arguments, people told us that the marriage age for young women has risen, stayed the same, or fallen. The most common explanation for a rise in the marriage age of women is that their situation is dependent on young men. Some told us, however, that even though men postpone marriage, they still prefer to marry younger women. As a woman ages, she is less desirable, and thus less likely to be proposed to. For her, as well, this creates a hardship as she fails to reach the basic hallmark of femininity and independence – and will likely suffer psychological and social consequences as a result. Listen to these three farmers from a remote *colline* in Ruhororo.

The only difference between young women and young men is that a girl my age does not have much of a chance to get married anymore. Whereas a young man can do it at any age. (Thirty-four-year-old man)

The marriage age has increased a lot! As a result, girls become old without ever finding a husband, and boys engage in illegal cohabitation. (Twenty-two-year-old woman)

For girls it is even worse because the crisis has killed more men than women and hence the number of women exceeds the number of men. Also, if a girl goes beyond twenty years, it is rare that she can easily find a candidate, if she hasn't studied. Boys prefer the least old girls. (Nineteen-year-old man)

This respondent touched upon a point brought up by several: one of the effects of the war has been a loss of significant numbers of men, which limits marriage possibilities for young women. The war created not only a surplus of young, single women, but also a substantial number of widows. In the face of competition, and with young men struggling to come up with enough resources to marry, women may be more willing than previously to enter into unofficial marriages or even polygamy to avoid remaining single. This thirty-year-old widow from Ruhororo told us:

> As a widow, I would like to remarry but it is difficult to find a husband in this period after the war. Look around you, and observe for yourself, that here in this marshland it is basically exclusively women cultivating. Who would marry a widow when there are so many girls who don't easily find a husband?

Widows are clearly one of the most disadvantaged groups in Burundian society. We heard sad stories of widows abused by family members, ostracized by their communities, losing access to land, and living in destitution.

We also heard repeated references to unmarried and married men having covert relations with widows – a way to have sexual relations with a woman without having the financial responsibility of marriage. A group of young men from the Ruhororo IDP camp explained to us, 'sometimes men see [a euphemism for having sexual relations with] a widow in her own house, but they would not build a second house for her. Widows often have relations with married men, because they need to financially.' Widows, financially vulnerable, are less desirable for having already been married and are not given the same level of respect as unmarried young women.

In Ngozi, there were a handful of participants who explained that the marriage age for young women is falling. In Bujumbura, this perspective was unanimous. The explanation provided is that young women agree to marry earlier (sometimes before the legal age of eighteen, and often unofficially) in an attempt to improve their dire financial situations. The following are from participants in Bujumbura:

> Young women live pretty much like young men (very poor). There are those who want to escape this life by all means, even prostitution. Others marry very young to be protected by a husband. (Twenty-four-year-old male, Musaga)

> Poverty brings girls to marry very young. Their lives change because when they need something their husbands are there to give it to them. (Eighteen-year-old male, Musaga)

> I had to marry very young because life was difficult at home without my parents. (Twenty-year-old female, Kamenge)

In short, while the marriage age for men has risen, there is good evidence to suggest that this is not the case for women. The effects of the war on marriage are different for men and women as well. For both, the war created further impoverishment, making it hard to lead the lives they socially value. This is especially painful for men, as their entire self-worth is caught up in being able to provide for a family. But the war does not seem to be the only driving force in these changes: rather, economic impoverishment and the decline in land availability are the crucial drivers, and as a result major regional variations exist between those areas where land scarcity is not (yet) a major problem and those where it is.

Burundian society also seems rather flexible in its capacity to face up to this new given. Men marry later, and there seem to be few social sanctions on that – people understand. But there are more mechanisms at work. The requirements for marriage are being relaxed as well. Many young men told us that instead of building a new house, for example, it was enough to add a room to one's parents' house – a far cheaper proposition. Many others said that informal marriage, saving on the costs associated with marriage, was on the rise, and generally socially accepted. The widespread availability of these options for many men may mean that the dynamic observed in West Africa does not occur in Burundi: young men are not systematically excluded from the relationships market to the profit of old men, and there is thus less of a generational or sexual conflict that might feed into civil war.

It can be argued that men drew benefits from the war in terms of their position in the marriage market: there are many more women available now, both young and not so young, including widows, and men are more powerful than ever in dictating the terms of their relations with women, especially in the city, where social control is weak. This includes polygamy, sexual relations with widows or with students, affairs with other women, and so on. It is clear that the costs of this accommodation are borne by women, who find themselves in tenuous relations or with no protection at all.

Upholding tradition: young men and young women The following section will take a closer look at the answers given to our expectations questions: 'What makes a "good" young woman or young man, what is expected of daughters and sons? What do you look for when choosing a spouse?' The majority of these answers are in line with what is understood as traditional masculine and feminine ideals throughout Africa.

With regard to young men, the majority of responses clustered around a set of connected themes: young men are expected to earn money, work hard, get married, and, foremost, support their parents, wife, and children.

> My wife expects that I as a man work hard and fulfill the needs of the family. I must be responsible and make the right moves at the right moment. For example, as the school year is about to start again I must already start thinking of buying books and uniforms for my children. (Twenty-eight-year-old male migrant, Nyanza-Lac)

> My parents expect me to create a family and have children and provide them with a solid basis for living, that is to say have a stable and reliable income source. (Twenty-eight-year-old self-demobilized soldier, Kamenge)

133

TABLE 6.1 Traditional expectations of young men and young women

Expectations	Young men	Young women	Non-gender-specified	Total
Support parents/ spouse/children	55	7	15	77
Work hard	24	36	3	63
Be obedient	25	22	15	62
Marry	23	14	12	49
Be polite/respect	9	28	9	46
Have morality	16	25	4	45
Earn money	28	0	11	39
Responsible	13	16	4	33
Do housework	2*	14	0	16
Stay close to home	5	4	2	11

Note: * These two young men (from different regions) said that housework is supposed to be done by girls, but in families with no girls – such as theirs – housework has to be undertaken by boys.

In short, the first dictate of a man's life is to work and be a provider (Turner 2004). This traditional set of values regarding male responsibility was the most frequently named expectation in urban and rural areas, by men and by women, by youth and by adults. This sheds light on the deep capitalist attitude we discussed in the previous chapter – this sense of never giving up on working hard, trying to make it, taking individual responsibility: what is at stake here for young men is not only their physical survival but their very social identity and dignity. It also acts as a reminder that masculinity leads first and foremost to responsibility – not to violence.

Another group of answers clearly describes a second major stream of expectations of young men, namely to be 'obedient,' 'polite,' 'have morality,' and 'stay close to home.' These expectations relate to young men's relations with family, and especially parents. They are the traditional values of good behavior. This set of values was much more prevalent in rural areas than in the city: morality, for example, was mentioned in 18 percent of the answers in the countryside but in only 1 percent in the city; for obedience the scores were 15 percent versus 3 percent. Clearly, then, this second stream of values is subject to social change: in the city, it seems, it is eroding.

Expectations regarding young women are similar to those for young men, but they are prioritized differently. For young women, the stream of values of obedience, moral behavior, and politeness and respectfulness comes first. The proportions of answers centering on 'obedience' and on 'morality' are three times higher for women than for men; 'politeness and respectfulness' score six times higher. Listening to parents, coming home on time, not hanging out with boys, and, more generally, sexual chastity and virtuous behavior – these come up over and over in the conversations. These values were spoken of in equal proportions by male and female interviewees as well as by those over and under the age of thirty, indicating that they are deeply internalized within society and not subject to much change. The main differentiation, again, is between rural areas and the city. 'Obedience,' for example, was mentioned for women by 35 percent of interviewees in rural areas and 20 percent in urban ones, and pretty much the same proportions prevailed for morality. Hence, as with men, it seems that expectations of women are being challenged by urbanization and migration.

The second stream of expectations about young women mirrors the first one concerning men. It deals with marriage, hard work, and household work. There are some fascinating insights to be found in this stream. To earn money, for example, is the second-biggest category for young (urban) men; yet it is not once mentioned as an expectation for young women – even though, as a straightforward matter of fact, many women clearly do earn money, both in the rural areas and in the city. Women earning money seems the ultimate taboo. Taking charge of the needs of parents, spouse, or children was mentioned at least fifty-five times for men, but only seven times for women – although, once again, women often play predominant roles in this. At the same time, 'hard work' is by far the top category of expectations for women, especially in the city (19 percent versus 9 percent in rural areas). Traditional gender expectations about women's work and the value attached to it remain widely pervasive.

In short, the Burundians we interviewed appear heavily imbued with traditional masculine and feminine ideals, even after a decade of war. Families may have been uprooted, the economy may be in a shambles, men and women may have had to take on different roles – but the expectations Burundians have of men and women still appear very much traditional, although expectations of traditional morality are declining in the city, especially for men but also, to a lesser extent, for women.

Moving away from traditional expectations

At the same time, there was a sizeable group among our interviewees whose answers to our questions about gender expectations ran against the stream, challenging traditional gender roles. This section picks up on these counter-trends. We focus on three main areas: women's education, dynamism, and spousal respect

TABLE 6.2 Expectations of young men and young women: frequency of responses based on 260 participants

Expectations	Young men	Young women	Non-gender-specified	Total
Education	39	52	73	164
Dynamism	12	23	3	38
Spousal respect and cooperation	20	22	NA	42

and cooperation. What we describe here is much less often discussed in the general literature on gender in Africa.

Young women and education One important result of our interviews is that in Burundi education is valued as much *for* boys as for girls (by their parents), as much *by* boys as by girls. And our data confirm this interview result: gender has no impact in any of the regressions we tried. Men do not have a higher educational attainment than women do, nor do they value education more; similarly, they do not desire it more for their boys than for their girls. This finding is particularly interesting because it contradicts most literature on women's education in sub-Saharan Africa. Quantitative data show that girls are under-represented in primary, secondary and tertiary schools, and have substantially higher rates of illiteracy in comparison to boys (UNESCO 2000). Qualitative research suggests that parents are unwilling to invest in a young girl's education for many reasons: they tend to place greater emphasis on the education of sons, who will likely attain higher levels of employment than daughters; girls need to work at home and take care of young siblings, farming, and collecting fuel; girls may become pregnant and thus be forced to end schooling, etc. (Kwesiga 2002; Yahya-Othman 2000: 35; Okeke 2001: 236–9).

Our conversations in Burundi differ significantly from this picture. While these factors all remain relevant to Burundi, our study clearly indicates that the expected gender backlash in educational access is not taking place in the country. Literally *all* our interviewees, regardless of category, stressed the importance of educating both young men *and* young women. In addition, when speaking about trends since the time of their parents, several young women described women's increased access to education as a positive change. This sixteen-year-old female student from the IDP camp reflected the sentiment of many: 'When my mother was young, women only did household duties and did not go to school, but because of development girls can go to school and get knowledge and skills.' Fathers – or future fathers – wanted their daughters to study. This eighteen-year-old Busiga farmer states it well: 'My daughter, I want her to complete her studies and engage in things that will help to prepare her for the future. If she is not able to complete her studies, she will get married at the proper age, i.e. not too young.' And educated men, both urban and rural, desire to marry women who have attained a certain level of education as well (although none of them wants to marry a woman with a higher education level than himself!).

The data in the previous chapter confirm this social change: education rates for young women are much higher than for older women, and in some places, such as the IDP camp in Ruhororo, girls' education levels were very high. Nyanza-Lac, a fertile region, used to be widely known for the low importance families attached to the education of boys and, even more so, of girls, but following the war a dramatic change has occurred here as well – and the rise in average girls' education was especially noteworthy. Generally, this trend results from the growing realization among Burundians that agriculture has no future and that education constitutes the best path toward a different life. The war has not dented this trend – indeed, among some people such as IDPs and refugees, it seems to have facilitated it.

Dynamism and young people Thirty-eight different interviewees described 'dynamism' as a positive characteristic of young people – whether they were talking about whom they wanted to marry or what they expected of their children. Dynamism refers to a set of personal attributes such as having foresight, being innovative, and/or actively seeking opportunities. It may not be surprising that dynamism is valued when describing young men – it seems to fit quite easily with a value attached to making money, to being responsible and in charge, all the more so in a society where competition for survival is cut-throat. What *is* surprising, however, is that dynamism was spoken of as a positive attribute for *women* three to four times more often than for men. We believe that our interviewees, when talking about dynamic women, were explicitly and self-consciously departing from traditional gender expectations. Those who spoke about the importance of female dynamism were slightly more often from Bujumbura than from the rural areas, slightly more often under the age of thirty, and more likely to be male. Here are some examples of how dynamism was described for women:

> I want to marry a dynamic woman who would not sit down and say, 'I will wait for what my husband gives me.' With such a woman, even if I am not rich, we can search for ways of getting better in life. (Twenty-two-year-old man, Ruhororo)

> My future wife, if I am lucky enough to get one, should be dynamic and smart to help me well in life and be a real partner in my life, not just be beautiful of body. It is of no importance if she is urban or rural. (Twenty-three-year-old male self-demobilized soldier, Kamenge)

> I want a wife who is full of initiatives and creative. She must be my right arm in the household, especially to search to improve the family well-being. (Forty-four-year-old male, Bujumbura)

In our interviews, it was especially young men – when describing a potential spouse – who valued dynamism. This desire is an adaptation to economic crisis: they know how hard it will be to survive, let alone flourish, as a household relying only on their own meager chances for income, and they seek a spouse who will take initiative, help out. This is confirmed by CARE staff, who did a series of intensive dialogues with women throughout the country. They argue that it is principally in the poorest households that women possess more decision-making power and that husbands talk favorably about their wives' independence (CARE-Burundi 2006: 5). Anthropologists have documented the same dynamics in Asian countries such as India and Bangladesh: families who can afford it do all they can to maintain traditional purity – poorer families, on the other hand, cannot afford these practices, and women are de facto much more 'liberated' there. This is exactly the analysis of this nineteen-year-old woman in Busiga: 'Girls are more dynamic and clearsighted now, because they can no longer count on their parents and their husbands. This is especially the case for poor girls, because the richer ones are taken care of by their parents.' The willingness of men to acknowledge that this is taking place is of interest here, suggesting that a change in gender roles is occurring. This change, as always, has as its starting point what exists – in this case the traditional expectation that the role of a woman is to work hard – but it does add an extra twist, valuing initiative and autonomy. Dynamism was more frequently emphasized as a desirable trait in women than in men. This may be for a combination of reasons. First, it may be generally assumed that young men need to be dynamic to survive: this is so evident it requires no specific mention. This is certainly not the case for women, however, and those who spoke of female dynamism made an explicit point – we think they were deliberately moving away from traditional gender roles in their expectations and attitudes. The novelty is of course not that women have suddenly become dynamic in Burundi, but rather that this dynamism is explicitly appreciated or recognized. Gender roles are changing in Burundi, then, as a result of the pressures of impoverishment.

Spousal respect and cooperation Another somewhat nontraditional response to the question 'What makes a good wife or good husband?' emphasizes the need to respect and to cooperate with one's spouse. For example, a thirty-year-old widow in Ruhororo told us, 'I would like to marry a man who treats me with respect, like my first husband. Also, I would like to find consensus on our future projects together.' A nineteen-year-old male migrant in Musaga said, 'I want a wife with whom I can discuss the problems of the household – someone who is comprehensive and who loves to work the land.' This was deemed an almost equally important trait for husbands as for wives; and it was mentioned by male interviewees as much as by females (16 percent of all marriage answers for both). Interestingly, the majority who spoke about this were under thirty; it was also mentioned twice as frequently in Bujumbura than in the rural areas. We believe that what we term 'spousal respect' and the emphasis on collaboration, discussion, initiative, and plain and simple respect may be the marker of significant (and thus by definition slow) change in the more traditional relationship standards in Burundi, especially among the younger generation. Perhaps such shifts serve as adaptations to increasing economic hardship – this may explain, again, why men mention this as well. Perhaps it is the result of longer-term social dynamics toward values of equality and equity, similar to what we documented in the chapter on citizenship.

The answers discussed so far in this section run counter to the relentlessly negative tone of so much scholarship on gender, in which, it seems, all men, when they have difficulty reaching masculine ideals, simply drop their responsibilities and take their frustration out on women (Silberschmidt 2001; Barker and Ricardo 2006; Amuyunzu-Nyamongo and Francis 2006). This is also of practical importance, as it offers levers for further, internally driven change. These young men and women we spoke to, after all, are not intellectuals or foreigners, brandishing the banners of feminism and the high moral ground. They are ordinary people, who have an impact on their neighbors and communities. Intelligent work with them can have a much higher pay-off than countless declarations and workshops in the capital.

Conclusion

The story of men and women in Burundi both converges and diverges from the existing literature on gender in sub-Saharan

Africa. Burundians identify with traditional African constructions of masculinity and femininity – at their core, to be a good young woman is to behave morally, to be a hard worker in the home of first her parents and then her husband, and to bear children. To be a good young man is to be financially viable enough to secure a marriage, support one's family, and provide for one's parents. And everyone ought to respect their parents and elders. Some of these values are beginning to change, especially for men in urban areas.

After a decade of civil war and many more years of population pressure and economic stagnation, young women and men find it very hard to live up to these expectations. There is near-consensus that young men find it very hard to marry in the way desired by themselves and their community. Some particularly vulnerable groups of young men simply declare that it has become impossible for them to do so.

This gap between the ideal – i.e. early marriage and a life as provider for a growing family – and the attainable has been described in many other studies as the cause of psychological problems, violence, alcoholism and drug abuse, as well as familial rejection and community ostracism (Silberschmidt 2001; Amuyunzu-Nyamongo and Francis 2006; Barker and Ricardo 2006: 161, 177). It is a common assumption nowadays that part of the popular appeal of participation in civil wars among young men results from the fact that becoming a soldier can give young men the prestige they fail to get through the regular path of marriage, and access to sex they cannot get conventionally.[3]

Some people we spoke to seemed to fit this picture. Among the young men we interviewed, some of the most depressed were those in the IDP camp in Ruhororo. (Note that, in this very camp, we found the highest average educational attainment for women – above nine years in our sample.) Living under social and economic trauma caused by the war and economically stuck in IDP camps, they are incapable of achieving normative manhood. A high proportion of them told us they expected never to marry. They adhered to some of the most misogynistic attitudes toward women we met anywhere: the labeling of women as prostitutes was a recurrent theme – those women who migrated, those with possible careers, those who strayed from tradition. One could thus argue that they responded by looking down on women in order to restore their compromised masculine identities.

On the flip side, a group of young men who were perhaps even worse off consisted of the self-demobilized ex-combatants we interviewed in Bujumbura. They felt they had sacrificed the best years of their lives for nothing; they are almost all unemployed, extremely poor, socially marginal, and unmarried. But these same people also all told us of their wish to marry the mothers of their children, to support their families. They spoke of integrity, partnership, responsibility – a mixture of old and new gender values and the values embedded in the institution of *bashingantahe*.

The primary reason why the strong link identified in the literature between economic hardship, the difficulty of attaining normative masculinity, and participation in violence does not hold in Burundi is, we believe, the already discussed flexibility of Burundian society. Our conversations show that young people and their families everywhere are devising adaptations – including migration, the widespread acceptance of unofficial marriage, and the general lowering of marriage requirements, and far bigger investments in education for both boys and girls – in order to manage the hardships involved in assuring economic survival and creating better lives (including attaining the marriage ideal). Such adaptations are changing both the institution of marriage and traditional gender roles. They make it less likely that 'frustrated masculinity' is a major driver of popular political violence in Burundi.

As usual, there is a lot of variation. Take the rural-to-urban migrants, for example, who see themselves as hard-working fighters, trying to make it in a tough world, and who often had marriage at the center of their life goals. Some gave us the traditional argument of wanting a wife from the countryside, for only they have good morals and work hard, whereas those from the city only want to spend money. But others talked with passion about desiring a wife who would be a partner, dynamic, creative, resourceful.

There was as much variation in the young women we interviewed. Some tenaciously held to traditional norms, but others pushed gender roles. With encouragement from parents, many of them study longer – far longer – than their parents ever did. Others are creative from a young age: they trade, they work in rural factories, they take leadership roles in cooperatives, they get elected to the *conseil de colline*. Many of them push boundaries in the private sphere as well. They negotiate different relations with their spouses – more freedom to move and work, more decision-making power within the household, more visibility and respect in the public sphere. And those who succeed share the tricks with their younger sisters afterwards!

Of course, many women have suffered as well, especially during these war years: they have been raped by combatants, beaten by their husbands, left behind by their boyfriends, kicked out of school when pregnant. Some are left with little choice but prostitution, or becoming a concubine, in order to survive. In a society where violence has become omnipresent, where the law does not function, and where frustration and anger are everywhere, it is actually amazing that all this does not occur even more frequently.

The scholarly and operational literature on gender and (post)-conflict would do well to pay more attention to the dynamics described in this chapter. Discussions of spousal respect and cooperation, of valuing education and dynamism in a young woman, are nearly non-existent in the literature. While these notions are certainly not desired (and even less practiced) by everyone in Burundi, they do represent strands in society, partly caused by the war, partly the result of longer-standing dynamics of economic impoverishment and modernization. They can be built on, but for that they need to be recognized.

7 | Justice, silence, and social capital

ANN NEE AND PETER UVIN

In the past fifteen years, the reach and expectations of transitional justice have expanded remarkably. As described in Ruti Teitel's genealogy, transitional justice has moved 'from the exception to the norm,' and entered a third phase of development where it is 'all transitional justice, all the time' (Teitel 2003: 71). According to a 2004 UN Secretary-General report, transitional justice incorporates 'the full range of processes and mechanisms associated with a society's attempts to come to terms with the legacy of large-scale past abuses, in order to ensure accountability, serve justice and achieve reconciliation,' including 'individual prosecutions, reparations, truth-seeking, institutional reform, vetting and dismissals' (paras 4, 9). Transitional justice initiatives thus encompass a broad range of interventions that vary in their emphases on punishment versus reconciliation; international versus national primacy; individual versus community focus; and formal versus traditional procedures. But orthodox transitional justice proposals all share the assumptions that punishing 'perpetrators' and establishing 'truth' are the only good responses following mass violence.

These assumptions deserve closer examination. Whether the orthodox transitional justice model of prosecutions and truth commissions can be transplanted from the political transitions where it developed (South Africa; El Salvador) to the community-based violence settings (such as in Burundi) where it is now applied is unclear.

The core of the transitional justice paradigm is rooted in Western values promoting punishment of individuals who have engaged in criminal behavior, based on full information, formal procedures, and legal reasoning. More recently, truth commissions – although less strong in fulfilling the ideal of justice – have also come to hold a prized position (Kritz 1995; Minow 1999). Support by the international community for establishing truth commissions in transitional periods has become almost a reflex. There has been a widespread belief that deterrence through punishment and reconciliation through truth-telling are universally valid, transcending specific abuses, conflicts, or cultures.

Burundi is no exception to this trend. At the end of its twelve-year civil war, the government and the international community that constitutes its financial backbone are formally committed to both an 'International Judicial Commission of Inquiry' (later modified into a domestic 'Special Chamber for War Crimes') that will prosecute those who committed 'genocide, war crimes and other crimes against humanity' and a National Truth and Reconciliation Commission (NTRC) that will be 'responsible for clarifying the entire history of Burundi, going as far back as possible in order to inform Burundians about their past. The purpose of this clarification exercise shall be to rewrite Burundi's history so that all Burundians can interpret it in the same way' (Protocol I, articles 6–8 of the Arusha agreement). The United Nations has sent a large number of missions to the country to advance this agenda; donors and international NGOs discuss it constantly. This is a major change compared to the past: no one has ever been convicted in Burundi for political murder (Reyntjens 1995: 7).[1] Implementation of these initiatives, however, is very slow: the government of Burundi is clearly not much in haste to turn these ideas into reality.

This chapter presents the results of the research used so far in this book complemented by a qualitative study on perceptions of justice and reconciliation conducted by Ann Nee at the same time and in two of the same communes, Ruhororo and Nyanza-Lac.[2] The focus of this study was on soliciting ordinary community members' desires and beliefs regarding justice and reconciliation.

Prosecution and truth-telling

The most striking insight resulting from both studies is this: the majority of Burundians do not desire prosecutions or, to a lesser extent, truth-telling mechanisms. The larger, open-ended, non-justice-focused research shows clearly that, when people are not asked specific questions about such mechanisms, but are simply invited to talk about the past and the future, about the state and the community they live in, they almost never spontaneously express a desire for transitional justice. The smaller justice-focused survey demonstrates that, even where people are explicitly asked about the desirability of prosecutions and truth-telling mechanisms, the majority of respondents prefer that one or both of the mechanisms not be established. The sole exception was in the IDP camp in Ruhororo, one of the most polarized and divisive places in the country, where a majority of the inhabitants supported prosecutions.[3] Let us now discuss the results in more detail.

First, both studies showed that the majority of people express sentiments in favor of 'forgetting,' akin to a general pardon, rather than prosecution. Respondents in the justice-focused study gave multiple reasons for this. Many argued that because such large numbers of people of all ethnic groups committed crimes, nearly 'the entire population' would be in jeopardy of prosecution.

> We must pardon everyone because if not, it will be like we will have to punish all the population. We must pardon everyone because all ethnic groups did bad acts. (Thirty-eight-year-old female, Nyanza-Lac)

> Because they are also Burundian, we don't have anywhere else to put them, so we have to simply forgive them to have peace. Since all groups acted in the crisis, it is truly impossible to punish everyone. We risk punishing the entire population. (Forty-six-year-old male, returned IDP, Ruhororo)

> People who committed crimes must be pardoned because killing them is not the best solution, for they also lost members of their families. So this would become very serious indeed if we tried

to kill everyone who killed someone else. (Twenty-three-year-old female, Hutu, Ruhororo)

If I look in the two groups, there have been errors everywhere, it is better to forget. If we try to look for criminals, we will find almost everyone is a criminal. Even if a person did not actually kill someone, I am sure that one day in his heart, everyone wanted to kill someone. (Twenty-three-year-old female, Hutu, Ruhororo)

Other respondents argued that a pardon is better because it would enable the country to look toward constructing a future instead of dwelling on the past.

For those who committed crimes, we must educate them. We must show them that what they did is not good. Then they will change and become more like us and can help to rebuild the country. (Forty-four-year-old female farmer, Ruhororo IDP camp)

We have already forgiven the people who hurt us. It is necessary for all Burundians to forgive so we can reconstruct the country. If we don't forgive and forget this will never happen. (Sixty-year-old female, Ruhororo)

If we continue to punish those who committed crimes in the past during the crisis, no one will feel at ease. For example, years could pass, and sometimes, even if you are innocent, people could accuse you of using lies. To alleviate things, it must be done, we must pardon them. No one is infallible. And even the person who did not actually kill someone, he thought about it. (Thirty-five-year-old civil servant, Hutu, Ruhororo)

An amnesty is the best solution for Burundi to try to begin a new life, a new page in the history of our country. (Thirty-eight-year-old woman, Nyanza-Lac)

Still others emphasized that prosecutions and truth-telling could not undo what had happened. They often repeated the same image: the dead won't come back, so what would be the point?

You can have lost your belongings and your family, but what will you gain if you stay angry? You are not going to see again the people you lost. (Forty-eight-year-old male, returned IDP, Ruhororo)

Even if I had access to justice, there would be no benefit because you cannot have back the people who have been lost. (Thirty-nine-year-old female farmer, Nyanza-Lac)

As for telling the truth, if we had meetings together, it is not worthwhile to say all that happened because people will not get anything for the people that they lost. (Seventy-year-old traditional *mushingantahe*, returned 1993 refugee, Nyanza-Lac)

My family – my wife and my six children – was killed. I know who did it. I sometimes meet them in the street: they greet me and I greet them. I have forgiven them: they can never bring back my family, so it is the best thing to do. It is best to forget and to get on with life. (Forty-two-year-old ex-combatant, CNDD, now *chef de colline*, Nyanza-Lac)

Second, in our research, the situation in Ruhororo differed sharply from other places in its attitude toward prosecution and truth-telling. In Ruhororo – a town deeply divided along ethnic lines, with a long history of violence and continuing distrust – the majority Hutu position (when obliged to express an opinion: recall that people generally do not talk about this if not explicitly asked) supported truth-telling and opposed prosecutions, whereas the Tutsi position overwhelmingly supported prosecutions and opposed truth-telling.[4] This clearly relates to how these groups politically interpret the civil war. Many Tutsi see themselves as the innocent victims of genocidal attacks. This is a fear they have grown up with for decades; the events of 1993, followed by their continued displacement (they were all still living in the IDP camp), are the daily proof of the reality of that genocide. They tend to want punishment for the perpetrators, period. Truth-telling is unnecessary in the face of such proof, and could simply become a forum for their aggressors to blame them for their own misfortunes or to bring their own grievances against the Tutsi, obscuring the weight of the crimes committed. Many Hutu, on the other hand, tend to see the last twelve years as a civil war for equal rights, a necessary fight against a system of social exclusion that had prevailed for decades and in which they were the victims. When asked about the desirability of various transitional mechanisms, therefore, they largely expressed a preference for a truth commission to clear up the past.

Another factor is the perception of the ethnic nature of the justice system itself. Hutu are suspicious of prosecutions because most of those imprisoned during the war were Hutu from the *collines*, and because the legal system in Burundi has historically been (and still primarily is) composed of Tutsi. Third, at the end of the civil war, Hutu have emerged the 'victors,' with a Hutu president and the integration of Hutu into the army, and prosecutions could upset these gains. In short, then, what justice means – and the approach to justice selected – is a highly politicized matter in a deeply divided community like Ruhororo, and, in all likelihood, among highly politicized people everywhere.

We do not believe this degree of politicization is common to all of Burundi. Most respondents everywhere, Hutu and Tutsi, declared that they preferred to forget. At the same time, we do believe that this politicization of justice does lurk just below the surface everywhere – in situations where antagonism mounts, or where people are presented squarely and directly with questions on the issue (as in our justice survey), they tend to revert to an ethnically based interpretation of justice.

Turning to the (Tutsi) IDPs in Ruhororo, the prime reason given for their support of prosecutions was the simple, forceful axiom that those who killed should also be killed. Without prosecutions, they further warned, the perpetrators would continue committing crimes, tensions between groups would continue to be aggravated, and popular vengeance could take over. In this group, opinions supporting prosecutions and punishment were often linked with strong, negative opinions against the recent liberation of the political prisoners.

For me, you must kill those who committed crimes because they also did not want that the others should live [...] To improve justice, it is necessary that the government take seriously the question of people who committed crimes, because if these people are not punished, they will repeat the same acts, and the IDPs who had accused them will become laughing stocks before these criminals. (Thirty-seven-year-old female, IDP camp, Ruhororo)

If someone commits a crime, he needs to be put in a public place and killed, as an example. If we kill criminals, there is no negative consequence to this. Because if someone kills, he needs to be killed. [...] There is the issue with the prisoners who were freed with the new [government]. If someone killed a person and is liberated and comes back to the village, you understand that they are not being punished for the crime. This makes people scared because it shows that you can repeat the same things. (Thirty-six-year-old male, IDP camp, Ruhororo)

Only two respondents in the IDP camp volunteered the idea that guilty parties on both sides should be treated equally in prosecutions. Both of these were *bashingantahe*, one traditional and one elected.

These people should be prosecuted by the justice system, which will determine their punishments. For me, if someone committed a crime, he must be killed, because he took a life. [...] I think amnesty is not a good solution. It will aggravate the situation if you see someone who killed your relatives without punishment. You will always be angered. [...] Criminals in both groups should be prosecuted in the same way. All groups of people committed crimes, and for the same crime, there should be the same punishment. (Fifty-four-year-old man, elected *mushingantahe*, Ruhororo IDP camp)

The rarity of this qualification from those who were in favor of prosecutions is surprising, in comparison to the prevalence of such comments from those who favored pardons. It suggests that the majority of those in the camp did not particularly consider that IDPs would also likely be implicated in any prosecution effort.

In Nyanza-Lac, where the patterns of violence have been different from those in Ruhororo, the responses in favor of prosecutions were far fewer; they also had a different quality. There were still individuals against amnesty because of the normative need to punish murder, in order to learn the truth of what happened, or to prevent a continuation of conflict. Respondents were much less in favor of the death penalty, however, and more in favor of using prosecutions to separate the innocent from the guilty, and as a future deterrent.

> The punishment of these people should be fixed by the law. We must prosecute people to know who committed crimes and who did not. Amnesty has created problems because people killed others and committed crimes, and if they are not punished, it shows that this will continue. (Thirty-nine-year-old woman, Nyanza-Lac)

> For criminals, I think they should get life in prison. For someone who dared to take the life of another person, they must not be allowed to live a normal life as if they did nothing. Even the life of a goat or a little animal has value; you cannot kill as you want. And even if you imprisoned criminals, but only those of one ethnic group, that would be another injustice. (Seventy-year-old female, returned 1972 refugee, Nyanza-Lac)

The most popular rationale given by individuals who supported truth-telling was that it would prevent a recurrence of the crisis. Paradoxically, a major reason invoked by people who preferred *not* to talk about the past was that doing so would lead to increased conflict.

> Yes, people talk about the crisis. It is not a problem to talk about the past. What would be bad would be to begin again to commit these acts. Talking about it is a means of avoiding a return of violence. (Twenty-three-year-old male, Hutu, Ruhororo)

If we don't find a way to talk and for the criminals to accept what they did, there will be rancor. This means that the ethnic conflicts will not really have ended. (Thirty-eight-year-old male, returned IDP, Tutsi, Ruhororo)

We talk about the facts of what happened, but we do not know what to do to prevent these things from repeating because there was another crisis in '93. If possible, it would be good to have meetings with the populations about both crises. Then we could talk about this [prevention]. (Forty-five-year-old male, returned 1972 and 1993 refugee, Hutu, Nyanza-Lac)

If we wrote everything that happened, that would be bad, because these acts must not be remembered. I find that if we return to go over all the past, there will be people who would be angry because we will remind them again of the unhappiness they have lived. If you need reconciliation, that means to forget all that happened. (Forty-year-old woman, Nyanza-Lac)

We must not talk about the crisis because we understand that these times are over, and because of fear that it might start again. (Fifty-four-year-old male, elected *mushingantahe*, Tutsi, IDP camp, Ruhororo)

Those who talk about the past are those who still feel rancor. They talk about the past to show that they have not forgiven the others and that they still have this rancor. (Twenty-three-year-old female, Hutu, Ruhororo)

Part of this contradiction seems to arise through the difference between talking about the facts of the past and talking about their origins. Talking about the facts is about suffering and loss, destruction and displacement. It can be therapeutic. It can have the power to create bonds, as so much of the suffering is so similar. It can facilitate coexistence. On the other hand, talking about the causes of the war – and a fortiori assigning blame, naming and punishing individuals – is divisive, as people differ profoundly in how they view these matters, and often have an interested stake in the outcome. The frequent position against talking about the past – and the assumption that doing so may cause fresh conflict – follows from the fact that many people realize that there are major divisions among them in how they see the past; as a result, these people fear that talking about the past would lead to accusations and blame.

> People do talk of the crisis, but they do not want to touch on the origins because if they do, everyone will start throwing around blame. Each ethnic group will think the other started it, and it will mire people's hearts in anger. I think that talking of the crisis should only be of the lives they lived while displaced, but not to evoke the subject of the origin [of the crisis]. (Thirty-eight-year-old female, Nyanza-Lac)

> Yes, there are divergent opinions about the crisis between different ethnic groups. For example, there are disagreements about the origin of the crisis. Both groups were responsible for killing members of the other group, but people accuse only the other group of killing. (Twenty-three-year-old male, Hutu, Ruhororo)

Our conversations revealed many more reasons why the majority of Burundians prefer neither prosecution not truth-telling but forgetting, moving on – amnesty, if you wish. First, Burundi is a society where justice in a full, blind, equal-for-all version has not existed for decades. People have no belief that any judicial solution proposed to them will actually work as promised, and thus may opt against any solution that requires a correctly functioning justice system. One could therefore argue that their responses do not prove that Burundians do not prefer Western-style transitional justice: it may be that they would really desire the full transitional justice menu, if they believed they had a fair shot of actually getting it, but that they are cynical that it will ever come about.

> As someone who is one of the common people, I do not know how to respond to the question of whether people should be prosecuted. When I try to comprehend that, until now, the case

of the assassination of the president [Ndadaye] has remained unsolved, like it has been thrown away, how can I imagine, if the killer of a president is not prosecuted, that the case of a simple peasant who was killed will be prosecuted? (Seventy-year-old male, traditional *mushingantahe*, returned 1993 refugee, Nyanza-Lac)

For me, if I met someone who did something bad to me, if we had a justice system, I could bring this person before the tribunal and the law would know how to punish this person. But there is no justice system here to study the question of punishment. (Seventy-year-old woman, returned 1972 refugee, Hutu, Nyanza-Lac)

But the effect of a historical absence of rule of law or of the sort of legal tradition that underlies the transitional justice agenda is felt in deeper, more socially anchored ways as well. In a context where rule of law and faith in any institution of justice are absent, people have developed many other time-tested strategies for survival that strongly caution against placing faith in formal justice mechanisms. Many of these strategies are predicated on silence, on letting go, on forgetting – by the widow who now finds a measure of stability in the house of a man who killed her family; by the young woman who, by never talking about her rape, can find a husband; by the men who, by not bringing up the past, manage to work side by side in a cooperative. Ordinary Burundians are by necessity highly pragmatic – it is only the well off, or those living abroad, who can afford principle. Many perceive that there is little chance of having meaningful justice and little practical benefit to it anyway, and they must focus their efforts on getting by in other ways.

Second, Burundians do have a fine understanding of how the violence of the civil war spread among them. In our conversations, people frequently hinted at the fact that a lot of the violence they were part of was committed out of fear. Both in the city and in the countryside, waves of insecurity rolled over the population, wiping out all normality. Many people ended up being both victims and perpetrators in this climate of fear. They may have committed horrendous acts, which do not represent who they normally are or aspire to be. Many came to regret these acts later. People naturally have a hard time confronting or talking about this, and trials, with their exactness, public nature, limited scope, and single-minded focus on culpability, may simply not be the best tools for resolving what happened in people's lives during these awful years of insecurity and fear.

Related to this, some of those who favored pardons conveyed their view that the war was a time that was wholly outside of cognizable human experience. The incomprehensibility of the acts committed went to prove that the people who committed them were not themselves and could thus not be held entirely to account for their actions. Others also used this idea as a reason why they would personally forgive those who had harmed them during the war.

> As for people in armed groups, all the people in this time were animated by a satanic spirit. They have had time to change their behavior. (Thirty-five-year-old woman, Nyanza-Lac)

> For these people who continue to want vengeance, they also do not have peace. We must not prosecute them, but we should engage these people to try to re-educate them. It is like they are not part of society anymore, they just dream of doing bad things. We must educate them to change their behavior. (Fifty-nine-year-old woman, returned 1972 refugee, Nyanza-Lac)

Third, Burundians everywhere consider 'the politicians' to be responsible for the war: they talk about being manipulated by politicians who come at night in black Mercedes, of gangs of criminals being paid by politicians to fan the flames of violence, of unreliable politicians in Bujumbura cynically using the masses in their fight for personal benefits. This sense that the politicians are to blame is one of the most widespread opinions about the war, shared by Hutu and Tutsi. Some people who favored prosecutions, consequently, told us that the politicians should be the first, or even the only ones, to be prosecuted. These responses correspond with the transitional justice principle of prosecuting those 'most responsible' for crimes, and may provide an indication that limited prosecutions in the proposed special chamber for Burundi might have some popular backing. Conversely, as described below, others responded that, despite their culpability, politicians should still not be prosecuted if a threat to the peace might result.

Most of these people who committed crimes were misled by politicians. They only executed what politicians said to do. We must forgive them and not prosecute them because it was not their fault but that of the politicians. (Forty-six-year-old male, returned IDP, Ruhororo)

The common people are the pillars of the politicians, they support the politicians in their bad works. If they don't have bad politicians then the people won't do it again. Most people have only executed the orders of the politicians, like innocents. If we prosecute and punish the leaders, then the others should be pardoned. [...] The first thing to do is for the International Court of Justice to begin work in the country. They must start with the high politicians, from all groups. It will not be possible to do this if these politicians remain in power, because otherwise it would already have started. It is a problem for the common people because the politicians see far and know that if the court starts its work, they will be accused and punished. So they do not want the court to start work. (Sixty-seven-year-old male, traditional *mushingantahe*, Tutsi, IDP camp, Ruhororo)

We must start first with the politicians; the crisis was born with the politicians. The politicians are more guilty than those who committed the acts. Those who committed the acts only followed orders. The politicians are very bad. Now, there are not bad words among the population; there is peace. But if the politicians were to come and teach bad things to the population, the population will always be there to carry out orders. (Forty-

157

nine-year-old male, elected *mushingantahe*, Tutsi, IDP camp, Ruhororo)

This widespread insistence on politician responsibility, with the correlative characterization of the population as having only mistakenly, unwillingly, or unwittingly been tricked into following orders, has multiple effects. In the present, it favors daily coexistence, by downplaying the personal responsibility of *all* people. This is consistent with a strategy of forgetting, and of not talking about the past – in both cases it allows people to move on, to re-create the social relations that allow them to cope with their forced interdependence. The impact of this widespread analysis on *future* violence is harder to determine. On the one hand, recognition of the role of politicians in manipulating ethnicity to instigate conflict seems to be a welcome antidote to their ability to do so again. This is, indeed, how many people presented it themselves: *now we know we have been tricked, and it will not happen again*; or *next time they come and tell us to kill, we will ask them to do it first!* A side effect of this analysis is of course that it effectively allows individuals to avoid closely examining their own behaviors and motives during the years of violence.

A fourth reason given by people who opposed prosecutions and truth-telling is a fear of endangering the transition. Indeed, in all places where we did research, among ordinary people and intellectuals, people repeated that the prosecution of politicians should be subordinate to the objective of maintaining security and peace.

Peace is necessary for simple country people – to cultivate, to eat, to have security. If the politicians are not prosecuted but there is peace, then I don't understand why people insist on punishing the politicians. (Forty-six-year-old male, returned IDP, Tutsi, Ruhororo)

Whether or not people who were leaders should be prosecuted is a question for the government. If they find that they should do it, they will do it. If they decide to pardon everyone, we all would be in agreement with that, so that the crisis will not restart. (Seventy-year-old male, traditional *mushingantahe*, returned 1993 refugee, Nyanza-Lac)

Burundians – both Hutu and Tutsi – are pleased with the transition: it brought them peace and a potential for development; for Hutu, it also created a more representative and stable system of government than anything they had known since independence. Full accountability of the key people involved in crimes could very conceivably undermine the transition. People high in the current elected government, the army and the parliament, as well as still-powerful outsiders, would have to face trial. It is unlikely they would do so voluntarily, and their resistance could very well destroy the transition and reignite civil war. People clearly value security far higher than justice.

Many of our interviewees also seemed to display a normative preference in favor of silence, as opposed to the more practical or instrumental arguments presented so far. Indeed, quite a number of people treated the desire to talk about the past almost as a weakness. People talk about the past, the argument goes, because they cannot help it, because they cannot stop themselves, because they cannot forget. It would be better if they could avoid doing so.

> We talk about the past when we get together, when we drink. We do not talk about why it started but of the sorrows we suffered. If possible, we must be silent, we should not speak on the subject of the *crise*. Why should we continue talking about it when talking about it is not important? (Fifty-five-year-old male, Nyanza-Lac)

> For me, I don't think it is good to talk about the past. But you cannot forget the periods of sorrow in your life. You can't forget those years. I don't know what to do if you have memories of bad things in your heart. But if you do talk, you need to only talk about what happened to you and that you don't want it to happen again. (Twenty-one-year-old man, Nyanza-Lac)

It is not good to talk about this because there were lots of losses and we must not remind people of all that happened. We must forget everything that happened to start another life. If people came and said we should get together and tell our stories, I don't think it would be good. (Thirty-nine-year-old female, Nyanza-Lac)

We believe some of this is due to cultural preferences of Burundians in favor of letting go of the past, of focusing on moving on, of being 'flexible,' as they sometimes call it. After years of anarchy and a weak state, people developed instinctive protective mechanisms for not speaking up or revealing the truth when it may lead to personal danger or conflicts. Compounding this is the atmosphere of lack of social trust that has come out of a history of state-led communal violence. Before any genuine truth-telling can take place, a minimum level of trust – with agents of the justice system as well as among community members – must exist. Truth-telling does not create trust, but can only follow it.

Even if [different ethnic groups] came together to talk about the crisis, there would be no trust. If the people talked together they would not speak the truth because of the lack of trust. When they left, the people would say different things than they said when they were together. (Fifty-five-year-old male, IDP camp, Ruhororo)

A national truth process will not be helpful. We Burundians are afraid to tell the truth. We think, if I tell the truth, I may be killed. Any process must be based on personal-level trust. Lack of personal trust now is key. If a process comes from above, it will create fear. (Male employee of UN agency, Tutsi, IDP camp, Ruhororo)

It would not be possible to put different groups together to talk. Even if we did put them together, they would not pronounce these feelings of desire for vengeance. (Fifty-nine-year-old female, returned 1972 refugee, Nyanza-Lac)

The problem with the [truth commission] is to find those who will be members of the commission. It is always a problem of politics – everyone is biased in one direction or the other. You will never find someone who can be in the middle between the two groups. (Sixty-seven-year-old traditional *mushingantahe*, IDP camp, Ruhororo)

This research also revealed a widespread desire for some kind of conflict resolution dialogues among Burundians – something which seems at first sight to contrast with the disfavor of truth mechanisms and preference for silence. Individuals frequently positively described mechanisms that were local, face-to-face, but not designed for truth and justice. Instead, these mechanisms focused on diffusing tension, interpersonal healing, forgiveness, and cohabitation. In short, they seemed to have in mind the sort of things that conflict resolution agencies like Search for Common Ground and others (as well as some engaged communal administrators) do in Burundi – not what is being described in the transitional justice literature. As we suggested earlier, one feature that may distinguish these mechanisms is that Burundians prefer efforts that help them find ways to live together again, rather than seeking to establish root causes or apportioning blame. Sharing mutual fears and re-establishing points of commonality in non-confrontational settings were seen as ways of fostering greater empathy. Several people stated that, in re-establishing trust on the individual level, they would feel even less of a necessity for prosecutions or truth-telling. The asking and giving of forgiveness that would be a prerequisite for trust would also accomplish the end goals of transitional justice, without the dangers inherent in a formalized process. Nevertheless, even in these responses, the underlying assumption was still frequently that it would be the responsibility of members of the *other* side to initiate such exchanges.

I have never heard displaced and *colline* residents talking about the crisis together. If the *administrateur communal* decided to have meetings to talk about these things, then that would be good. If someone else, for instance in the site, wanted to start talking about it, it would be good because it would be a means of reconciliation. To talk with sincerity about all we lived during the crisis could open the hearts of people, and make them accept to reconcile. (Twenty-two-year-old female, Hutu, Ruhororo)

If someone asked my forgiveness, I would be ready to forgive this person. The idea of being satisfied by this is my idea, though, not for everyone. If I forgave a person, I would prefer that he not be prosecuted by the justice system, or that the justice system also pardoned this person. But the forgiveness would depend on how he explained himself, and on the dialogue that we would have. After this forgiveness, trust and relations would be reborn between these people and me and I would not be afraid of these people anymore. (Twenty-seven-year-old male, Ruhororo IDP camp)

For those who were friends before, we talk about the crisis, not about the origins but the facts. For example, we talk about life in the refugee camp, in the site, in the bush, and those who stayed in the village. When we talk, it is like everyone tells their story, then they add that there are no ethnic killings or divisions. They say that their friends must warn them if it is going to happen again. (Forty-year-old woman, Nyanza-Lac)

It would be good if people got together to talk [in mixed groups], each could air his feelings. This fear of return can be erased by conversations. (Forty-six-year-old male, returned IDP, Ruhororo)

The last, and very important, reason why most Burundians do not prefer the available transitional justice menu is that they overwhelmingly think of themselves as having moved beyond ethnicity and division. In our broader research, we asked people how *entente* was in their lives. The word is hard to render in English: it refers to notions of getting along, living without friction – cohabitation or coexistence may be the best term (Chayes and Minow 2003).

In these conversations, the overwhelming majority of people everywhere in Burundi were very positive about the state of *entente* in their neighborhoods or *collines*. Whether in rural or in urban

TABLE 7.1 Attitudes toward *entente*

	Entente is good now	*Entente* is still a problem
Busiga	18	0
Ruhororo camp	6	5
Ruhororo *colline*	1	0
Nyanza-Lac	8	0
Musaga	45	0
Kamenge	27	2*
Bwiza	16	0
Other urban	18	0

Note: * Both are FNL self-demobs who clearly felt ill at ease in their communities, for they could still face retaliation from either the FNL or the army for their past actions, if neighbors informed on them.

areas, poor or rich, almost everyone we spoke to made a similar argument when asked about *entente*, namely: '*entente* is good here, for we all live the same problems.' As we all share the same structural conditions, they told us, we realize that ethnic divisions do not serve us. Of course, there are conflicts in households and between neighbors, we were informed, but nothing that can't be solved *à l'amiable* (in a friendly manner).

Once again, the only place where a different situation prevailed is the IDP camp in Ruhororo, where a significant number of people in the larger study said *entente* was not good. This limited exceptionalism in the IDP camp was not a reflection of a broader Tutsi reflex. We interviewed many Tutsi throughout the country (the urban commune of Musaga, for example, is almost entirely Tutsi), and yet it is only in the Ruhororo IDP camp that a sizeable proportion of interviewees differed from the general position. This suggests, once again, that much of what we heard in the IDP camp in Ruhororo is a reflection of isolation and trauma. The people there live separated – a well-defined island of Tutsi in what many of them still perceive as a hostile sea of Hutu.

The people living in the IDP camp in Ruhororo were generally among the most depressed people we met during our months of talking to Burundians. The weeks spent in the camp talking to its inhabitants had a palpable heaviness. Older people fear their former neighbors, bemoan their lost children, their loneliness, their displacement. The young people had no hopes for life: no work, no capacity to get married, no access to credit, no professional training. Separation, trauma from the pogroms of 1993, and ongoing social and economic constraints, then, seem to combine to explain the differential results of the people living in the IDP camp.

Even with some qualification, this result is an important one, for it informs us of some crucial dynamics in Burundi. One is that the current political situation of the country favors ethnic reconciliation, or maybe more precisely a letting go of ethnicity. Contrary to what happened in the past, all political parties go out of their way to not present themselves as representing ethnic groups, and officials speak about Burundians rather than of Hutu or Tutsi. The second is that this answer, even if factually incorrect, reflects an image people consider desirable. After all, Burundi is not a dictatorship like neighboring Rwanda, where every word can be overheard and reported back to intelligence services and where only one single state-imposed discourse is allowed. Hence, even if this overwhelming answer that *entente* is good is an image projected at outsiders, it is at least one that has widespread grounding in society, reflecting how Burundians like to think of themselves – or present themselves – after twelve years of brutal ethnic civil war.

Also illustrative of this desire to see their society as beyond ethnicity were responses to the question 'Whom do you admire?' A large number of answers consisted of people describing to us ordinary acts of justness and conflict resolution, or actions to defend others, all of which were special because they happened *across ethnic lines*. Stories like these comfort people, it seems, and demonstrate to all that a page has been turned, can be turned.

I admire a professor at his college communal. Someone wanted to unjustly send a student out of school: this professor defended the student with the administration, even though he was of a different ethnicity than the student. (Nineteen-year-old male student, IDP camp, Ruhororo)

I admire the one who has given me my job. He did it without knowing me or knowing my ethnic or familial background. (Twenty-four-year-old self-demob, security officer, Musaga)

I admire someone who discriminates against no one. Who acts for the good of others. In the IDP camp there was a *chef* like that. He intervened in a difficult situation to witness and save the life of a neighbor who was unjustly accused, even though he was from the other ethnic group. (Nineteen-year-old female farmer, Nyanza-Lac)

I admire my Hutu neighbors in my *colline* of birth. They remained *solidaire* when I lost my parents. (Thirty-seven-year-old man, Tutsi, private sector employee, Bujumbura)

I admire people who hid others [during the crisis], their neighbors and friends. They saved their lives. I also admire IDPs in the camp who, when they heard there would be an attack on the *collines*, went to warn you so you could flee. (Twenty-five-year-old woman, Hutu, Ruhororo)

These statements perfectly reveal the dual truth about Burundi: Burundians clearly admire this sort of behavior and identify with it, spontaneously so, but, equally clearly, this behavior is rare – that is precisely why it is a source of admiration. These stories do refer to past divisiveness, but they focus primarily on surmounting ethnicity. This sentiment corresponds with study results showing a desire to avoid transitional justice mechanisms in order to avoid recalling directly the dangerous ethnic rhetoric of the past. In constructing a society that is beyond ethnicity, Burundians may rightly see such a beginning as undesirable, unnecessary, and a threat. But there is more.

One of the most striking observations emerging from our research in Burundi is the way people constantly maintain some form of relations across great chasms of violence, class, abuse, and absence. People have civil relations with the murderers of their families; husbands and wives, even after many years, can reconnect and share all again; refugees and IDPs return home, solving their own land conflicts in the process. And all of this happens against a background of stunning poverty. Burundi specialists decry the level of land conflicts, involving as many as 9 percent of all households in the province of Makamba, a center of return of refugees and IDPs: in many areas, as much as 80 percent of the current population consists of people who have just returned during the last few years. But this still means that an amazing 91 percent of the population is *not* party to any land conflict, and this in a country where every square foot of land is a matter of life and death.[5] Let's not forget: throughout the country, this means Hutu and Tutsi are living side by side again, for they were intermingled everywhere. How, then, do people manage to such an extent to reintegrate, after a decade of war, dislocation, and poverty?

This puzzle becomes all the more perplexing as Burundi does not have any public rituals, mechanisms, or procedures of community reintegration or reconciliation. Not one Burundian, whether intellectual or peasant, Hutu or Tutsi, urban or rural, described to us any ceremony or rite of reintegration or reconciliation, whether traditional, religious, or state-sponsored. While there are some local conflict resolution initiatives, more often people described the total lack of any recognized formal or coordinated efforts. Instead, the process leading to cohabitation takes place ad hoc at the individual level. In the areas where we worked, with the exception of the Ruhororo IDP camp, people seem to just return and arrange themselves with neighbors.

Burundians themselves talk about flexibility when they describe how this happens. What they mean by this is that they value the capacity to compromise, to go with the flow, to hide their true feelings, to move on. These are individual behaviors, anchored not in deep community-based mechanisms, but rather in the essential *individual* struggle for survival of all Burundians. At the same time, these attitudes and behaviors are socially valued: Burundians are proud of this, and uphold it as desirable.

There seems no doubt that this results from Burundians' profound vulnerability: they need to maintain relations at all cost, for, apart from their bodies, the little bit of social capital they have is the only thing that may make the difference between total destitution and simple poverty, especially in a context of complete absence of rule of law. The capacity to maintain relations with people who crossed you, whom you distrust, is crucial, for one never knows – they may be necessary one day. Those who exploit you today may be at your mercy tomorrow and vice versa, but the only way to have a fighting chance is to stick with it. It is likely that this happens most from the perspective of women; it is they who depend upon and invest in these relations most.

This, then, is not the Putnamian social capital of generalized trust born out of collaboration and compromise, shared norms and expectations. Rather, it is based on such an extent of generalized, institutionalized, and internalized *distrust* (as well as insecurity and absence of rule of law) that one needs to build up the maximum amount possible, in order to survive. In a situation of insecurity and unpredictability, and in the absence of community-based mechanisms of reintegration and reconciliation, Burundians protect themselves by nurturing relations, by compromising, by maintaining a poker face under all conditions. None of them necessarily believes these relations are lasting or profound – indeed, they all know that they cannot trust each other's word, that beer shared today does not exclude betrayal tomorrow. And so the system reinforces itself, particularly in circumstances of uncertainty. This is a practice both of great integration and division, of stability and radical change.

The question of culture in all of this is fascinating and difficult. Burundians have long been described – and describe themselves – as masters of dissimulation, of not showing their true feelings. They are proud of it and will often jokingly tell you about the fact that you should never trust their words, that a no can always mean a yes and vice versa, that they can warmly hug the man they will kill a few hours later. They treat this as a cultural feature: this is how we Burundians have been since time immemorial, this is our culture. This theme is represented in a line of Burundian proverbs, such as 'the one who doesn't lie has no food for his children.' This sort of behavior – the language, the body gestures, the strategic choices, the expectations – is reproduced through the generations, passed on from parents who demonstrate this behavior and probably also glorify or a least legitimize it to their children. As such, it becomes normal, invisible – just as our own Western constructs and expectations are largely invisible to our-selves. As a result, dissimulation and the constant maintenance of social capital at all costs are repertoires Burundians are very well qualified to use, and which serve them well. This strategy is necessarily mixed with culture; it is a culturally appropriate response to a set of issues Burundians face in their lives.

The potential for traditional transitional justice mechanisms to be divisive and to unravel the ties that form the basis of this social capital is evident. In accusing or testifying against neigh-bors, individuals would break with the socially preferred silence and risk ostracism, suspicion, and reprisal, as well as heightening ethnic animosity in their communities and elevating barriers to the cooperation on which their survival depends. As such, sup-porting these mechanisms would be an act against individuals' immediate and long-term interests, in a context where most of the non-elite have nothing to spare.

Conclusion

Our conversations reveal two strong tendencies that run coun-ter to the basic tenets of transitional justice. First, most people seem to prefer to forget, to be silent, to draw a veil over the past, whether out of fear, shame, a sense of futility, a normative preference in favor of silence and flexibility, or – most likely – a combination of these factors. This preference has deep cultural and socio-economic roots that go far beyond the strict transitional justice debate and relate to how people have learned to cope with extreme uncertainty, poverty, and upheaval. Second, the paradigm of prosecution and equal treatment for the same acts, no matter who committed them, is not shared by many Burundians. Most people on both sides see themselves as victims and the other as aggressors; each sees its own acts as necessary for survival while the other group's acts are patently unjust. When people talk about wanting justice, then, they more often than not intend it to be meted out for the crimes committed by the other side. When they speak of forgiveness, most foresee that it is the other side that ought to be apologizing first. For many people, in short, to the extent that they desire justice, they see it through a politicized lens. The more polarized the situation, the more people revert to this distorted approach to justice.

Both these factors together strongly suggest that only a minority of Burundians adhere to the notion of justice as consisting of impartial prosecutions, nor do many more believe in the need for the full truth, known to all, about all events. In simpler terms still, the norms presumed in the international transitional justice agenda have little purchase in Burundi.

This also runs counter to the dominant diagnostic about the problems in moving toward transitional justice in post-conflict countries: the implicit assumption by scholars and policy-makers is usually that 'the people' want justice (defined in the manner and form that the international community proposes), but that the power-holders block that deep groundswell in favor of justice by their short-sightedness, arrogance or fear. Our interviews in Burundi reveal that both the strong and the weak, the powerful and the powerless, prefer partial justice, or even silence and 'no justice.' Deep ambivalence toward transitional justice in Burundi exists not only at the level of the state, but also among the local population. Life goes on, and social and economic relations are re-established; beer is shared, as are benches in the church. This coexistence is a far cry from justice in any international meaning of the term but it is recognizable and, to some extent, desired, by people.

Our conversations also suggest that people do appreciate when safe environments are created for them to talk about the hardships they faced and the fears they still have, and to reach out to others in their communities. Dialogues and workshops along those lines, organized by communal administrators, parish priests, *bashingantahe*, and professional conflict resolution NGOs are widely liked – and there are far too few of them. These processes may lead to some measure of individual reconciliation and even forgiveness.

Finally, and as we saw in Chapter 5, Burundians want to be treated with equity and respect by the state, and they frequently talk about issues that Westerners would call 'rule of law.' There *is* in Burundi a social grounding to move toward justice as defined by the international community, then, but this process is a much slower and much more locally specific one than the transitional justice literature and practice seem willing to recognize.

8 | Conclusion[1]

In the following pages, I will present some final insights, building on the results from the conversations presented so far but also going beyond those, trying to tease out implications both more theoretical and more operationally relevant. I will start with some fresh insights about the causes of war in Burundi, and follow this with a discussion of the role of young men therein – one of the factors that motivated me to do this study. This, in turn, will lead to some ideas about gender and development in a post-conflict context. Broader discussions about citizenship and democracy at the end of violent conflict will end this chapter.

War

The arguments about the origin of civil war in Burundi that I will outline in the following pages differ from – and I believe nicely complement – existing explanations, which all focus on national-level elite competition for political power and its attendant advantages (e.g. Ndkimumana 2005; Lemarchand 1996; Prunier 1994; Reyntjens 1995). This dominant explanation is correct (and widely shared by Burundians as well) but additional elements are required to ground it – and to see the potential for change in Burundian society. These additional elements are, first, the dynamics of radicalization and deradicalization that Burundi has gone through; second, the role of local elites in spreading violence; third, the role of insecurity in creating the conditions for mass violence; and fourth, the real grievances of the majority of the population.

Radicalization For decades, Burundians have been caught in a totalizing process of redefinition, in which all people of the other ethnic groups increasingly came to be seen as (potential) enemies; preventive or pre-emptive self-defense became the only rational strategy (Uvin 1999). For Tutsi, this process started with the Rwandan 'social revolution' and continued with every violent action by Hutu soldiers or parties in either country. For Hutu, it began in 1972, with the mass murder of tens of thousands of Hutu intellectuals.

During those decades, on both sides, extremist political entrepreneurs became more credible, as they seemed to provide the best defense against the aggressive aims of the other side;[2] the ethnic division, not crucial to people's definition of self or to the political landscape at independence, became *the* fault line of socio-political life. The twelve-year civil war is the culmination of that: it truly was an ethnic war, and it divided towns, neighborhoods, and regions into ethnic warring camps. In many – but not all – towns and neighborhoods, broad-based ethnic cleansing took place; Hutu and Tutsi families fled in different directions; their sons tried to kill one another; newspapers discussed the deaths of only their own side. This was total ethnic war.

But this dynamic has begun to change. More and more Burundians have started redefining the enemy not as all people of the other ethnicity but as *extremists* on the other side, or even as *politicians* of all stripes. By 2006, this position represents the majority understanding of the cause of ethnic war in Burundi. This is a major – albeit reversible – social change, with potentially profound implications for conflict dynamics in Burundi.

What caused this change, and why was it different from what occurred in neighboring Rwanda? I can only offer some suggestions. Part of it may lie in Burundi's deep political culture, which has always had stronger elements of consociationalism and compromise than Rwanda's (Vandeginste 2006; Sullivan 2005) – whether in the early 1960s, in the early 1990s, or now, the Burundian political system has always tried to revert to a compromise-based and ethnically inclusive system of political governance. These systems have failed over and over, as centripetal forces took over, and the violence this has always unleashed has precisely contributed to the growing totalization of ethnicity and enmity described above. In comparison, Rwanda has always been a much more winner-take-all political culture. In both cases, it is possible to make parallels with the pre-colonial systems of governance (Lemarchand 1970).

Second, a profound and general cynicism and distrust toward the state have come to characterize Burundians: the state in Burundi is much weaker, more corrupt, more visibly exploitative, than in Rwanda, and no post-independence politicians have possessed the legitimacy or effectiveness that Kayibanda or Habyarimana had in Rwanda. My conversations show that this sense of alienation from politicians – including those of one's own ethnicity – has become dominant (with the exception of the person of President Nkurunziza at the time of my work), thus making it easier to cast the blame on them, to detach oneself from their words and actions, which have so often favored violence.

Third, with very few exceptions, all Burundians have suffered dramatically from the war. The stalemate was mutually hurting, not only militarily but also economically and socially. Violence, it seems, does not guarantee security in Burundi, does not protect people from depredation, does not make life better. Burundians gave war a chance, to quote Luttwak (1999), and saw that it does not pay. As security conditions improved significantly in much of the country from 2001 onwards, it became possible for people to be less caught up in the needs of individual and collective self-defense, to restore social relations, to reflect on the past. This is when my interviews took place.

Fourth, for a decade Burundi has seen a veritable explosion of conflict resolution activities: the country was in many ways the world's top laboratory for this sort of work – well-listened-to radio programs, constant seminars and training at the elite level, dialogues among ordinary people. It is hard to quantify the impact of this work on peace writ large, but it seems quite possible that some of it did actually pay off, especially in conjunction with other factors described above. More research is needed on this, including the role played by local conflict resolution actors – churches, NGOs, informal leaders.

Local elites I worked in two communes in the province of Ngozi. Busiga had remained rather untouched by the violence of 1993, while Ruhororo was torn apart in repeated spasms of internal violence. What explains these differences between two communes that are no more than 10 kilometers apart? There is not some dense, impenetrable tropical forest that separates them, preventing direct contact: decent roads exist, with Ngozi, the provincial capital, in the middle between these two. Neither is the cause separate historical dynamics or class structures – this region is totally homogenous in almost every respect. Rather, the explanation resides with the idiosyncratic relationships between local power-holders.

The differences between communes result entirely from the behavior – the aims, the ideologies, the power relations – of two small groups of local elites. The first group is composed of what one can broadly call the local administration and social elite. The communal administrator and various *chefs de zone* and *colline*, back then all nominated from above, are evidently in this group, but it also includes people like the directors of the local schools and hospitals, as well as some people not hired by the state: priests and monks, and the rare development professionals living locally. These educated and mostly administrative people act as the transmission belts between the center of the country, the government and the party (back then a single party), and the bases. They pass on the *mots d'ordre*, they control the population, they brief the higher levels on what is going on, who is malcontent and why. They truly are the crucial link between the center and the rest of the country. Whoever has the allegiance of these people controls the countryside (thus making local-level appointments a crucial matter not only of redistributing benefits to supporters, but also of ensuring political control over the territory).

Another group that influences local political dynamics is composed of the *ressortissants* – people who were born in the commune and have made it into senior positions in ministries, public enterprises, the UN or NGOs, and so on. Part of what these people do is simple development work. But they also engage in serious local political involvement and mobilization. Burundi's decentralization law explicitly allocates a significant proportion of positions on the communal council to this group – an open invitation for political aspirants to maintain local networks of patronage and clientelism, to undermine local democracy and downward accountability, and to spread political ideologies and competition from the center to the periphery – an invitation that many of them gladly accept.

It is in the competition and alliances between these small groups of local elites that communal politics unfolds. They buy off local intermediaries, drive into the hills at night and organize 'secret' meetings, distribute machetes and beer if serious violence needs to be organized, etc. They know who thinks what, who has a conflict with a neighbor from a different ethnicity, who is desperate for money – all levers of potential violence, should the need arise. This is the micro-politics of violence. It also means that it is crucial to involve these people in conflict resolution and leadership workshops: they, much more than the population at large, are the crucial sparks to light the fire of violence. Explicitly targeting local 'negative leaders' – local elites who are known to be extremist and exclusionary or simply powerful – is absolutely crucial in this respect: development practitioners tend to avoid these 'difficult' people, but the real need is to work with them.

Insecurity The third factor that is commonly misunderstood or neglected in discussions about civil war in Burundi is violence and chaos. A lot of the violence, whether rural or urban, was committed in a climate of fear, chaos, and insecurity. This statement sounds tautological but what it means is this: in societies where the rule of law is close to non-existent and security forces are neither effective nor trusted, small groups of people willing to use violence can create enough chaos and fear to force everyone into making violent choices.

In other words, it is not necessary that all of society partake in extremist ideologies for extremists to force all of society into awful, often de facto 'extremist,' choices. Most people will simply

175

flee, losing their meager possessions in the process. But many others will fight back to defend themselves and their families, will be tempted to opportunistically seek personal benefits, will become angry and strike back blindly, and so on – committing untold acts of so-called ethnic violence they would not have contemplated under normal circumstances. As an example, in our interviews the foremost cause ex-combatants gave us for why they joined rebellions, or the army, was fear and insecurity (Uvin 2007b). They had been attacked, they were afraid, school had been closed, they had fled and were without their parents. Many of these youths wanted to do other things with their lives but chaos and destruction – initially caused by a small group of people – turned their lives around. Many Burundians understand this: it is one of the reasons they do not necessarily want to discuss or punish all violent acts of the past, for they sense that things were done that people did not want to do, under extreme circumstances. Clearly, then, a law enforcement approach – the coercive imposition of order, as done by police forces, investigative units, the penal system – ought to be at the heart of conflict prevention, and it needs to work well before the chaos and violence become so widespread as to create a climate of fear. This is akin to the squeegee approach to law enforcement that was made famous by Rudy Giuliani when he was still chief of the New York police – the idea that, in order to bring down massive serious crime rates, you have to start with ending the many smaller crimes (things like jumping the metro, vandalism, intimidation), for they create a climate of fear and lawlessness that is conducive to serious crime. Note that these sorts of debates and activities are far beyond the comfort zone of the international development community.

Grievance So far we have treated the war in Burundi as a giant pogrom, an instance of mass violence – although one instrumentalized by elites, local and national, seeking their personal benefits. And part of the war in Burundi did display these characteristics: the pogroms against Tutsi after the murder of Ndadaye in many parts of the country, the ethnic cleansing of Bujumbura, and so on. But the civil war was also rooted in a rational political agenda, which was widely shared among many Hutu: the need to overthrow a regime and defeat an army that was widely seen as intent on maintaining exclusive control of the state and all the attendant benefits. One of the prime motivations for Burundian ex-combatants to have joined the rebels – the CNDD and the FNL – was a clear political agenda (discussed in more detail in Uvin 2007b). In my interviews, those who strongly identified with this agenda were more frequently (although by no means exclusively) older; they were also typically not the poorest or the most marginal.

These were people with political analyses and aims, who knew what they were doing. They voluntarily joined the fight,[3] and they won their war. That is also why many of them voluntarily demobilized: the job was done, and it was time to return home. It is likely for the same reason that the integration of these ex-combatants – whether child soldiers or adults – went very well: almost all of them moved back to the localities and families they came from and report no problems (ibid.). The war may at times have degenerated into banditry and crime, but that was not its aim, and for many soldiers and their families the general sense of mission did not disappear (Samii 2007 has detailed data on this subject). Burundi's civil war, then, was not based on the popular explanations of greed (Collier and Hoeffler 2001), natural resources, demography, or frustrated masculinity (Richards 2006).[4]

I draw two conclusions from this. First, each case is specific, and the general explanations that dominate international thinking about conflict in Africa must never be accepted at face value as universal explanations. At best they are general correlations, but they are surely not always true in the particular, even if the structural factors they are based on prevail in a particular country. The second, and more controversial, lesson I draw is, to state it as a slogan: structure is nothing, politics is everything. All the currently popular explanations for conflict in Africa focus on major structural factors – population density or age distribution; natural resource dependence; economic trends. But these factors explain nothing about why a conflict happens in a particular place at a particular time – and yet, as professionals of development and peace-building, that is what we need to know. Worse, they create the false feeling that we know what matters, which may lead to either false pessimism or false optimism. Hence, for a practice of conflict prevention, these theories are totally useless.

Masculinity and violence

The shock troops who commit most of this violence are typically composed of young men – not grannies. This brings us to the dominant model in the social sciences today, which we find expressed in very different ways, using different methodologies and causal relations, in the works of Paul Collier (with Hoeffler 2001), Robert Kaplan (1994), Paul Richards (2006), Gary Barker (2005), or Henrik Urdal (2004) – all of which largely treat young men as an imminent danger (Sommers 2007: 2; 2006b: 6). This image is very widespread in Burundi as well, both among ordinary people and among policy-makers: I recall an interview with the top person in the Department of Youth in Bujumbura, who repeatedly justified the need for more resources for youth programs in terms of criminality. He proudly told me that his minister had been successful in getting more funds for a youth employment plan by arguing to his fellow ministers that 'if you don't fund this, they will come into your houses to steal your possessions and rape your wives.'

This book has confirmed that many of the factors that scholars describe – joblessness, humiliation, incapacity to marry – do exist in Burundi. Where our analysis differs is in our understanding of the reaction of young men and the societies they live in toward these trends. When young men face great difficulty in achieving normative manhood, they do what most of us do when confronted with major challenges in our lives – they try harder than ever, they seek to innovate, they try to move and find opportunities elsewhere, they turn to God for strength, they hang out with friends and complain – but they do not necessarily become murderers. Burundian masculinity centers on responsibility – taking care of wife and children, as well as of parents. It is true that this definition devalues female contributions to the household, relegating them to the private and the invisible. But it is equally true that this masculinity is not automatically or even primarily violent.

The power of masculinity to explain civil war in Africa has been exaggerated in the scholarly literature so far. The overwhelming majority of young men in Burundi, as elsewhere, faced with the same poverty and thwarted masculinity, have chosen many life paths other than violence, even during the awful years of war (UNDP 2006b: 27ff.). Indeed, less than 3 percent of Burundian young men joined an armed movement during the war (see too Sommers 2007: 3; Barker 2005: 157, 181). Much of this literature on masculinity generalizes far beyond what is acceptable, as well as being overly 'miserabilizing.'

The relevance of the 'frustrated masculinity as a driver of violence' explanation is even more limited in terms of actual programming. Its primary policy implication is the notion that a focus on young men – through education and jobs – is a tool for conflict prevention. While this is certainly relevant – there is nothing young men and women want more than education and jobs – it is not a solid or actionable basis for conflict programming.

There exists no social science that can tell us precisely the identity of the young men who will take up arms, or engage in criminal and violent and destabilizing behavior. As said earlier, it takes only small numbers (and the political entrepreneurs who typically organize and equip them) to create a climate of fear and anarchy that is propitious to the spread of violence. Among the shock troops of violence, the young, the school leavers, the urban and peri-urban, those with disrupted or non-existent families (Brett and Specht 2004: 3), and ex-combatants are probably over-represented, but that still leaves hundreds of thousands of people to 'target' for conflict prevention activities. At the same time, the resources available are far from sufficient. Even if one

179

managed to lift a hundred, a thousand, or even ten thousand of these young men out of poverty – an amazing success few projects ever achieve – there will be many, many more who remain equally easy to mobilize or recruit, and many more who have received jobs but who would never have been recruited in the first place. In short, development assistance cannot prevent civil war by providing potential perpetrators of political violence with jobs. Creating jobs for youth *is* absolutely crucial for development, but it is not a useful conflict prevention tool.

If one wishes to use development funds in such a way as to reduce social dynamics leading to violence, other ideas are more promising. First, there is the already mentioned law enforcement approach, provided this can be done in a way that is impartial and legitimate – a tall order in any country. This was probably impossible in pre-war Burundi, given the composition and the record of the security apparatus. Now, with the integration of the army and police, there are many more possibilities, and this should be a priority for donors and the government.[5]

Second is improved local accountability: the spread of central-level conflict to the rest of the country takes place through the transmission belt of local elites of all stripes. Any process that increases the availability of information at the local level; that strengthens the habit and capacity of ordinary people to use the legal mechanisms available to control those who govern them; that empowers a broad range of informal and community leaders to act as intermediaries and alternatives to local elites – all these local governance mechanisms are conflict resolution tools in a country where people want to go beyond ethnicity and fear, but have precious few opportunities to learn how to make that happen.

Third: mechanisms and social processes by which central leaders are restrained from using violence as a key tool of doing politics by other means. Burundi has made great progress in this field: the emergence of a vibrant free press, as well as a much deeper awareness by ordinary citizens of the way they are being manipulated. But more can be done, including much more forceful diplomatic action by the international community when political leaders blatantly and consciously destabilize domestic political situations.

The fourth point is related to the first: improvements in economic and political fairness are crucial – the rule-of-law agenda, a tough nut to crack. Even at high levels of poverty, if ordinary citizens feel they have a fair chance of succeeding, they will maintain a stake in the system. Burundian youth are capitalists: they deeply believe in education, hard work, personal initiative, and individual responsibility. The general corruption and social exclusion (including through unequal access to higher education) offend them, make them cynical and angry, and make violence easier to justify or accept (Ndikumana 2005: 16). That is why the fight against corruption is a crucial element of a long-term conflict prevention strategy. From a conflict prevention perspective, more important and more doable than creating jobs, then, is to create a climate in which young people can believe that their hard work will pay off – no development, but also no peace, without institutional change.

Gender

Burundians' lives are profoundly changing under the tectonic pressures of continuous impoverishment and insecurity, reducing to rubble all that they held dear and thought would last for ever. Gender roles are no exception. Traditional expectations of men and women continue to make up the core of Burundian identity, even among young people. But they are extremely hard to achieve. Failure to achieve normative masculinity does leave young men unhappy and frustrated. And women's lives, both the joys and the sufferings, unfold in gendered ways as well.

But these same economic and political pressures are simultaneously unleashing different, opposing forces. These are dynamics wherein girls and women are encouraged to study as long as they can, where female dynamism and mutual respect between spouses are increasingly sought, where traditional marriage expectations are relaxed. This conforms to Barker and Ricardo

(2006) when they write that 'Various studies and research [...] confirm that many young men simultaneously hold traditional and rigid views about gender alongside newer ideas about women's equality.'

There is an excessive miserability in much of the masculinity literature. It resembles initial gender – read feminist – scholarship of a few decades ago. When scholars first focused on the situation of women in development a few decades ago, disaggregating women's experience from men's and trying to understand the way in which the social construction of gender impacts on social change, the result was overwhelmingly negative. It laid bare – for good reason – the plight of women, the gendered ways in which their experiences were not taken into account and how they often failed to benefit from so-called development. This early work was soon reproached on the ground that it neglected female agency and creativity and ongoing changes in society. A variation on this theme seems to be prevalent now that the gender focus has started to include masculinity. The new literature is extremely miserabilistic as well – men as suffering from economic crisis and social and political disempowerment. The difference is that these men, presumably, all take it out on others (or themselves). And, again, while much of what is said is true, this initial approach also neglects agency and change. The overwhelming majority of men do not turn violent. Faced with stunning constraints, they seek different ways to survive, to innovate, to find respect, and often in so doing some of them slowly begin reinterpreting gender roles as well – not without resistance, for sure, but appreciably none the less. In its relentless focus on violent behavior and its almost automatic association between young men and violence, the literature has – mostly unintentionally – created a picture that does injustice to the dignity of young men.

I argued that much of the social science scholarship is excessively miserabilistic (which would explain the difference between my results and those in the general scholarship), but it must also be acknowledged that Burundi differs from the other countries where much of this work was undertaken (primarily Sierra Leone and Liberia). Burundi seems more able to adapt to young men's inability to achieve normative manhood than other societies, and as a result young men's frustration and marginalization may be less severe than elsewhere. There are some good reasons why this might be so. Burundi is a much more non-hierarchical and amorphous society than most others in Africa and elsewhere, with no strong village chiefs who have the power to enforce rules, no initiation rites to maintain purity. Life has always been more individualistic and centered on the nuclear family than elsewhere, as the traditional dispersed mode of habitat graphically illustrates.[6] Second, Burundian society has always valued flexibility, the capacity to bend, but never break, to adapt to changing circumstances. And third, the civil war in Burundi actually had a major ideological aspect to it for most participants, who were defending the future of their people, and were widely seen as doing so by their communities. Perhaps these factors explain why young men in Burundi do not seem to conform as much to the 'young men equals frustration equals aggression' model that has come to dominate scholarship.

On a practical level, what this all means for aid agencies is that they can, and ought to, build on ongoing gender changes in society. Burundi presents a fertile terrain for a 'positive deviance' approach to social change, building on already ongoing dynamics. CARE-Burundi's work, using appreciative inquiry methods to uncover stories of significant personal and gender change (as determined by the women themselves, and not by outsiders) and then taking these women *and their husbands* to talk to other women about their experiences, is very interesting in this respect (CARE-Burundi 2007). Change exists, and it is carried from within. It does not need to be imported.

Peace

Our conversations clearly revealed how people defined peace in terms of law and order and an absence of criminality and banditry. The security dimension is *the* peace dividend people appreciate, across ethnic divisions and places. For most people, it is pretty much impossible – and irrelevant – to separate banditry committed by rebels or soldiers from banditry committed by ordinary criminals, or politically motivated plunder from economically motivated plunder. In both cases, the result is the same: you live in fear, and you risk losing your meager assets. This confirms the growing consensus that there is no development without (a sense of) security.

Another important conclusion is that there are significant differences in the extent to which Burundians have suffered from the war. Some places, such as Ruhororo and Kamenge, have been among the very worst hit by the war for many years and are full of people who carry deep personal traumas. Their suffering seems to be continuing after the war: there is more psychological trauma here, more anger, more economic hopelessness, less money to rebuild.

Agencies working in post-conflict countries need to target certain categories of people, if only because they have insufficient resources.[7] Rather than this targeting being done by accident, they can focus on certain categories. One possibility is to prioritize a particular group whose grievances and capabilities are such that it could constitute a menace to peace – the idea underlying DDR. One such group is the 'self-demobilized,' young people who spent years as child soldiers and who quit their troops (whether FAB, CNDD, or FNL) at some point – because they were wounded, sick of fighting, or afraid for their lives because of internal purges (Uvin 2007b). There are probably a few thousand such young men in the city (especially in Kamenge and Bujumbura rural). Their sense of having needlessly suffered, of being neglected by everyone, defines their lives, and their anger and frustration are palpable. They are prime recruitment terrain for any spoiler who wants to threaten the peace. Providing these people with a sense of future, a stake in the system, is a peace-building activity that falls eminently with the domain of development. Another possibility is to assist a group that has been disproportionately hurt by the war: starting with them may demonstrate that times have changed. One such group consists of young Tutsi men in the displacement camp in Ruhororo, mostly devoid of hope of any profitable economic activity, waiting all day for an opportunity that never comes, living surrounded by trauma and a sense of victimization. These are just examples, but they illustrate what a conflict-sensitive development strategy could fund. This is especially important for mechanisms such as the newly created Peace Building Fund, which was set up to do exactly that – but does not currently do so (Action Aid et al. 2007). These are tough choices that need to be made, and they ought to be made based on good information and clear criteria. This is hard in any political system, including a fragile and young one like Burundi's.

What is politically interesting about the two places that continue to suffer most from the effects of the war is that they are very dissimilar in terms of location and ethnicity. Ruhororo is totally rural, Kamenge urban; Ruhororo's IDP camp is inhabited by Tutsi only, whereas Kamenge is totally Hutu. This has broader political implications, both for donors and post-conflict governments – they can choose targeting strategies that send clear political messages and undermine extremist interpretations of post-conflict trends – and for the structural evolution of the political landscape: not all winners are of one ethnicity, nor are all losers. Coalitions are possible, and, indeed, did emerge in Burundi. This is a factor of hope for its further political evolution.

Development

Farming is a prison to most Burundians.[8] In the countryside, especially in the north and center, people desperately want to reduce their dependence on the land. The three big ways for young people to escape poverty are education, migration, and hard work. To Burundians, secondary education is crucial: the primary if not the sole image ordinary people have when thinking about an escape from poverty is that of the *fonctionnaire* – not a matter of public service but of individual gain. More generally, urban migration is the crucial way by which young people try to make a decent living for themselves and their families; it is a way to prepare the conditions for marriage as well.

185

In this respect the policy neglect of the city is alarmingly out of focus. There are understandable reasons for this neglect. First there is the traditional donor perception that poverty is rural only. This is blatantly wrong: the relations between the rural and the urban in Burundi are so dense that it is impossible to separate them, and many more rural people live off urban income than is acknowledged. Second, the current government clearly sees its power base as being in the countryside. This is good news, reversing decades of neglect and exploitation of the countryside under the previous regimes. But it is also dangerous and mistaken if taken to extremes. There is deep poverty in the city, as well as great potential. From a conflict prevention perspective, it is in the city that the conditions for violence are by far the most ripe: the dense concentration of ex-combatants, the deep frustration felt by many as a result of their relative impoverishment when compared to the visible wealth of the new elite, the presence of political entrepreneurs with deep pockets – all these factors facilitate further violence.

Burundians think of survival and progress in profoundly individualistic and capitalist terms. It has become common to argue that 'culture matters,' and this is often taken to mean that people in developing countries lack the cultural values that favor individual advancement and innovation. Talking to ordinary people, one is struck by the constant repetition of the themes of hard work, perseverance, good planning and foresight, and, increasingly, innovation and dynamism. It is impossible to over-estimate the value of perseverance in poor people's lives. Under all circumstances, dramatic setbacks occur for the poor; war makes this worse still. The capacity to fall and stand up again, to never give up, no matter how badly one is hurt, becomes essential for progress in life. Religion is crucial too, especially, it seems, in the city. It provides a value framework that allows people to persevere against all odds; a sense of dignity and community that are often absent in much of daily life; and a way to avoid the temptations – drinking, womanizing – that for the poor in Burundi can lead to total destitution.

This should, once and for all, lay to rest the 'dependency syndrome' argument in development circles. How many hundreds of times have I heard that argument, expressed by high-earning intellectuals, local and foreign: 'helping the poor is dangerous for they will become (or are already) dependent on aid'? Aid dependence, it seems, acts as an explanation for every negative social phenomenon. The rural road not maintained; the anti-erosion measure not adopted; the expression of hunger in a conversation – all due to aid dependence. Nonsense, and condescending nonsense at that.

Governance

All of Burundi's modern institutions (the ones the international community recognizes and interacts with) would cease to exist in their current form if it were not for foreign money. More than half the state's budget comes from aid, and, basically, so does the entire NGO sector's financial lifeline. Even the churches, the other major players in Burundi's social and economic landscape, could not survive without constant donations from abroad. Much of what exists in terms of modern enterprise – construction, restaurants, transport, banking – exists because of the physical presence of the international community. Aid represents 39 percent of GDP – almost twice the value of exports of goods and services. The 'modern' institutions of Burundi, then, are truly artificial: none of them can be sustained by internal resources and effort – nor have they domestically emerged or been negotiated among internal social forces. And yet, these are the only institutions with which the international community interacts. To make matters worse: the form these 'modern' institutions take hardly captures what truly takes place within them. This neo-patrimonialism – the capture of formally modern state institutions by neo-traditional, civil-society-based, patron-driven dynamics – has become the dominant lens through which the African state is conceived now (Erdmann and Engel 2007), and Burundi seems no exception.

But change is happening. The dynamics of the last decades

– including the violence – constitute the constantly evolving appropriation by Burundians of the 'modern' state they were suddenly bequeathed by the departing colonizer. In the early years, not surprisingly, the best connected and best armed took over the state machinery and used it to their advantage, while the large majority of Burundians neither knew what to expect nor complained. From their perspective, continuity prevailed in terms of the individuals who occupied the positions of authority and the sort of clientelist relations they maintained with these people. The new state was effectively reappropriated by the old political system (Laely 1997; Ziegler 1971).

But this did not last. First, from 1966 onwards, the highest levers of power were captured by a clan of low-caste Tutsi who previously would never have been able to amass such power and prestige. While the way the state interacted with the inhabitants of the territory changed little, this change in top personnel did slowly impact on state–society relations: the legitimacy of the system fell precipitately, and increasing amounts of naked oppression were required for the powers that be to maintain control. The state constantly lost legitimacy and effectiveness; it eventually fell apart in rapid economic decline and, finally, civil war.

Out of the ashes of the old, new dynamics are now starting to emerge. Ordinary people are angry about corruption and violence, about being misled, neglected, exploited, used and abused. They have come to profoundly distrust politicians and the state. The old system has lost its legitimacy. People demand respect, to be listened to, to be treated fairly and equitably – prototypes of human rights and citizenship, in other words (An-Na'im 1992). And the way the Arusha negotiations ended, with multi-party equilibrium, makes it harder to return to the *parti unique* of yore.

Add to this the fact that Burundians genuinely desire to move beyond ethnocentricity, and that, as we have documented throughout this book, distinctly different ideologies exist. Burundians have different opinions about the war, about the ethnic question, about marginal youth, social mobility, gender even.

What all of this suggests, then, is that even in an ethnically devastated society like Burundi, there exists a social basis for issue-based, non-ethnic politics. I believe there is a social grounding for an entirely different political practice in Burundi.

The mental image that Burundians use when talking about a new relation with the state and with each other is that of the deeply anchored and still socially valued institution of *bashingantahe* – the wise men whose impartiality, knowledge, and sense of justice are so widely accepted that they are chosen to advise in local conflicts. The institution is severely weakened now, but it remains the reference point for most Burundians. Many of the examples they gave us – of people they admired, of behaviors they desired, of standards they set for themselves and for others – described the attributes of a *mushingantahe*. This leads me to conclude that Burundians, when thinking about respect and equity and non-discrimination and justice, do not seek better institutions but better people. They demand the same end result sought by human rights activists – non-discrimination and dignity – but they do so not in terms of human rights, but rather of social relations.[9]

This poses a deep challenge to the development community. It always talks about participation and local ownership, but what if people have a completely different epistemological framework on matters of governance and justice – one that approaches these matters through the lens of social relations and personal attributes rather than structures and institutions? Surely this lens is hard to reconcile with the development business's usual obsession with institutional capacity-building and political neutrality.[10]

International aid does not recognize this nature of the political dynamics discussed here. It sticks to a formulaic, formal vision of democracy, both at the national and the local level. This vision is far removed from the understandings and concerns of most people. As a result, it cuts short on process, internal learning, and ownership; it is ultimately too easily subverted by the powerful, as has been proven by past experience.

Notes

1 *A brief political history*

1 The Rwandan Patriotic Front, a rebel movement born out of the Tutsi diaspora, which invaded Rwanda from Uganda in October 1990.

2 Arusha Peace and Reconciliation Agreement, Preamble, Protocol I.

3 But not CNDD/FDD, the biggest rebel movement by far. Nyerere had decided, in order to manage the negotiations, that split-offs from parties to the Arusha talks would not get a seat at the table, and as a result it was never represented.

4 These are early 2006 figures; the budget was subsequently revised in July 2006.

2 *Methodology and location*

1 I put him down as a repatriated refugee. I ended up creating a second category for everyone, and in that one I had him as internally displaced. At the end of the day, though, few answers to questions differed significantly between these categories. This may be because the key variables in Burundians' life are rather similar, and/or because the categorization, indeed, was too arbitrary and reductionist.

2 An indicator that can only be used in conjunction with others, for it applies both to the most well-off families, where someone has salaried employment, and the very poorest – the landless who survive only by working for others.

3 Uvin (2007b) teases out the results of these interviews only – something that is not repeated in this book.

4 The provincial average is 22 percent: CARE spreadsheet '*population totale ciblée par PACTDEV*', which mentions as its own source WFP's '*Etude sur la Vulnérabilité des ménages 2004.*'

3 *Peace and war*

1 Crucial comments were received from Adrien Tuyaga, Kimberly Howe, Craig Cohen, Benoit Birutegusa, Pie Ngendakumana, Joseph Bigirumwami, Kristiana Powell, and Noel Twagiramungu. I also got useful feedback from Susanna Campbell, Cheryll Hendricks, Antonio Donini, and Frédéric Clayé.

2 Galtung's work on 'structural violence' was part of that same debate (Galtung 1996; Lawler 1995). I took this up in my own work on development and conflict (Uvin 1998, 2003).

3 For example: in another

question – what would you do first if you became communal administrator? – the fight against delinquency was a frequent answer (see Table 4.1).

4 The results of my conversations with sixty-three excombatants, including seventeen 'self-demobilized,' can be found in Uvin 2007b.

5 It seems likely that, as Kristiana Powell observed, such notions of communal harmony can be used as tools for reconciliation.

6 See also Pouligny (2006: ch. 3) for an excellent discussion of this mindset.

7 Pouligny (2006) is very perceptive about the effects of this obsession with security and the class-biased nature of social interactions on UN mandates.

4 *Respect, corruption, and the state*

1 This chapter has benefited from important feedback from Kim Howe back when it really was a pain in the neck to read it. Great comments were also received from Cheyanne Church, Benoit Birutegusa, and Adrien Tuyaga.

2 Le Billon (2005: 73, 82) observes the exact same fact in surveys in the Balkans, Nicaragua and Sierra Leone.

3 The traditional form client-ship took in Burundi (*ubuhake*) was a patron's gift of cattle to a client, who, in return, had to perform labor for the patron and owed allegiance.

4 Largely the model described

by Mamdani (1996).

5 This is where we diverge from Chabal and Daloz, whose brush is too broad: the institutions they describe are much less legitimate than they are willing to recognize.

6 Note that what was mainly peaceful about these elections was the day they were held. There was significant intimidation before the elections, as the parties fought the CNDD/FDD (which possessed parallel administrations throughout most of the country) for local control. Afterwards, the usual mechanisms of cooptation and intimidation allowed further solidifying of power. Hence, democratic elections are sandwiched between non-democratic processes, but the international community needs only the day itself to allow itself to congratulate itself on its beautiful success.

7 OK, this is slightly overstated. Donors also support the media – indeed, Burundi's radios would not survive without foreign assistance. They also support a number of courageous or simply nice NGOs. This is largely positive: great people have been helped, and they have had real impacts. But even that remains a top-down approach, which neglects the deeper potential for change in Burundian society.

5 *Hard work and prostitution*

1 My thanks for comments by Kassie McIlvaine, Benoit Birutegusa, Liz McClintock.

2 Note that we also have a large number of people considering this a negative social trend, of course. There is no change without resistance.

3 In Musaga, eighteen out of nineteen who gave us positive answers were migrants, and so was the sole person who stated that his life was better than his parents' in Kamenge. Among the rich group, migrants were the dominant category too.

4 Note, however, that many of the better-educated refugee youth have not returned to Burundi yet, preferring to continue their studies, or get jobs, abroad. This affects these results.

5 Among our interviewees, the average child lost four years of schooling in rural areas.

6 Observatoire Urbain (2006: 98) documents that only 3–4 percent of the people from the neighborhoods we worked in has ever had contact with an NGO.

7 Twenty-three percent of all people living in Bujumbura households have no family tie with the head of the household (Observatoire Urban 2006: 30).

6 *Changing gender expectations*

1 We thank Benoit Birutegusa, Adrien Tuyaga, and Kassie McIlvaine for their fine comments.

2 This is not new: Trouwborst (1962: 139) already describes how 'permanent extra-matrimonial unions [...] often transform into legal marriages after transfer of a dowry.' But he goes on to add: 'Extra-matrimonial pregnancy of a young woman is strongly feared. In the old days, the guilty party could be killed and his father risked confiscation of his possessions. The only way to escape was to pay a high ransom.' This is not the case anymore, as such pregnancies are very common now.

3 For example, researchers have concluded that young men who failed to achieve acceptable constructions of masculinity were more likely to engage in conflicts in Liberia and Sierra Leone, participate in ethnic violence in Nigeria, and are more likely to be involved in violent gangs in South African townships, or were easy targets for recruitment by the genocidal Rwandan government. See also Barker and Ricardo (2006: 173); Sommers (2006a: 145, 153).

7 *Justice, silence, and social capital*

1 Burundi specialists argue that the culture of impunity that grew after each successive wave of violence led to increased tendencies both to use brutal violence in future repressions and to resort to vigilantism by those unable to obtain justice or protection by other means (Dexter and Ntahombaye 2005: 35).

2 The study was carried out in conjunction with Miparec, a Burundian NGO established to promote conflict resolution and reconciliation in local communities. The study consisted of

two-hour-long semi-structured interviews with thirty-five respondents in Ruhororo and eighteen respondents in Nyanza-Lac, primarily initiated based on random encounters within the selected communities.

3 See the discussion of differences in the IDP camp within the section on *entente*, below.

4 This mirroring dichotomy is in itself interesting, because prosecutions and speaking about the past were not offered as a binomial choice in our justice survey. Instead, respondents were asked what they thought of both, independently. While the literature says that 'truth' and 'justice' do not have to be preclusive of each other, our respondents in Ruhororo seem to have decided that they would be.

5 Admittedly, many of the toughest cases – refugees of 1972 – have not yet returned. Also, if the Land Commission, just created to solve these conflicts, fails to do a decent job, more conflicts could erupt.

8 *Conclusion*

1 I thank Kim Howe, Justin Ginnetti, and Marc Sommers for their comments.

2 See Chrétien (1990) for a good definition of extremism in Burundi.

3 The current image is always one of child soldiers being forced to fight, but that is not what I found in Burundi, nor is it generally correct (Brett and Specht 2004).

4 This may also help explain the low level of trauma I found (Uvin 2007b): research shows that youths who have had an active engagement in political struggle and/or ideological commitment are more resilient later (McEvoy-Levy 2001).

5 To their credit, it is: the PRSP, the PBC program, and general donor support have targeted the police and the army to an extent that would have been impossible even a decade ago. Comprehensive SSR, however, has proved very difficult so far.

6 Burundians do not live in villages but in isolated homesteads spread out throughout the entire countryside. Traditionally, neighbors live tens or hundreds of meters away from each other, and there is no central square, no baobab tree where the old meet daily to smoke and drink. People meet, of course, at markets and church services, but there is a lot more isolation here than elsewhere in Africa. Note that when I describe Burundi as flat, I am not talking about class or income: there are great inequalities in Burundian society.

7 The current categories of targeting are too vast to be of any use. Take a major community-based reconstruction project the World Bank just launched, for example: it defines the 'most vulnerable' groups the project will target as 'ex-combatants, displaced persons, youth, vulnerable children (orphans, ex-combatants,

street children, children heads of household), households affected by HIV/AIDS, women, elderly, disabled, Batwa population' (2006: 22) As much as three-quarters of Burundi's population falls into this category! If one wants to use aid as part of a peace-building strategy at the end of war, it will be necessary to do a much more fine-tuned analysis in order to fund those activities whose rapid implementation can have a crucial impact on peace consolidation.

8 I described this a decade ago for Rwanda: Uvin (1998).

9 We observed a similar redefinition of a Western concept in terms of social relations in the chapter on justice too.

10 I thank Justin Ginnetti for this insight.

Bibliography

Abrahamsen, T. and H. van der Merwe (2005) *Reconciliation through Amnesty?: Amnesty Applicants' Views of the South African Truth and Reconciliation Commission*, available at <www.csvr.org.za/papers/paptahv.htm>.

Action Aid, CAFOD and CARE (2007) *Consolidating the Peace? Views from Sierra Leone and Burundi on the PBC*, London, June.

Addison, T. (2003) *Africa's Recovery from Conflict: Making Peace Work for the Poor*, Helsinki: WIDER.

AFRISTAT (2005a) *Rapport de Présentation du système d'information pour le suivi des stratégies de lutte contre la pauvreté au Burundi*, Bujumbura, 12 January.

— (2005b) *Structure Indicative du Bilan Diagnostic de la Pauvreté au Burundi*, 12 January.

Agadjanian, J. (2002) 'Men doing women's work: masculinity and gender relations among street vendors in Maputo, Mozambique', *Journal of Men's Studies*, 10(3), cited in Barker and Ricardo (2006), p. 163.

Allman, J. (2001) 'Rounding up spinsters: arrest of unmarried women in the colonial Asante', in Dorothy Hodgson and Sheryl McCurdy (eds), *'Wicked' Women and the Reconfiguration of Gender in Africa*, Portsmouth, NH: Heinemann.

Alusala, N. (2005) 'Disarmament and the transition in Burundi: how soon?', Occasional Paper no. 97, Pretoria: Institute for Security Studies, <www.issafrica.org/pubs/papers/97/Paper97.htm>.

Amuyunzu-Nyamongo, M. and P. Francis (2006) 'Collapsing livelihoods and the crisis of masculinity in rural Kenya', in Ian Bannon and Maria Correia (eds), *The Other Half of Gender: Men's Issues in Development*, Washington, DC: World Bank.

An-Na'im, A. (1992) *Human Rights in Cross-Cultural Perspectives: A Quest for Consensus*, Philadelphia: University of Pennsylvania Press.

Annan, K. (2005) *In Larger Freedom: Towards Security, Development and Human Rights for All*, New York: United Nations.

Ball, N. (2001) *Human Security and Human Development: Linkages and Opportunities*, Report of a conference organized by the Programme for Strategic and International Studies, Geneva, 8–9 March.

Barker, G. (2005) *Dying to be Men: Youth, Masculinity and Social Exclusion*, New York: Routledge.

Barker, G. and C. Ricardo (2006) 'Young men and the construction of masculinity in sub-Saharan Africa: implications for HIV/AIDS, conflict and violence', in Ian Bannon and Maria Correia (eds), *The Other Half of Gender: Men's Issues in Development*, Washington, DC: World Bank.

Boyce, J. (2004) *The International Financial Institutions: Post-conflict Reconstruction and Peacebuilding Capacities*, Seminar on 'Strengthening the UN's Capacity on Civilian Crisis Management', UN Secretary-General's High-Level Panel on Threats, Challenges and Change, Copenhagen, 8–9 June.

Brachet, J. and H. Wolpe (2004) *Peace and Development in Burundi*, Washington, DC: World Bank.

Brett, R. and I. Specht (2004) *Young Soldiers: Why They Choose to Fight*, Geneva: International Labor Organization.

Burnel, P. (2006) *The Coherence of Democratic Peacebuilding*, Research Paper, Helsinki: WIDER.

Buzan, B. (2004) 'A reductionist, idealist notion that adds little analytical value', *Security Dialogue*, 35(3).

Call, C. T. (2007) 'Introduction', in Charles Call (ed.), *Constructing Justice and Security after War*, Washington, DC: USIP Press.

CARE-Burundi (2005a) *Programme d'Action Communautaire pour le Développement Durable (PACTDEV). Enquête de base*, March (team leader Linde Rachel).

— (2005b) *Consortium de l'initiative de sécurité des conditions de vie des ménages. Enquête de base*, September.

— (2006) *A Short Summary of Where We are with the Journey for the Strategic Impact Inquiry Review*, Bujumbura, September.

— (2007) *Empowering Approaches for Understanding Empowerment*, Bujumbura, June (written by Kristien de Boodt).

CENAP and NSI (2006) *Rapport du Sondage sur les Perceptions de l'Etat de la Sécurité et le Rôle des Corps de Défence et Securité au Burundi*, Bujumbura: Centre d'Alerte et de Prévention des Conflits (CENAP) and Institut Nord-Sud (NSI), December.

Chabal, Patrick and J. Daloz (1999) *Africa Works: Disorder as Political Instrument*, Bloomington: Indiana University Press.

Chambers, R. (1983) *Putting the Last First*, Harlow: Longman.

Chayes, A. and M. Minow (2003) *Imagine Coexistence: Restoring Humanity after Violent Ethnic Conflict*, New York: Jossey-Bass.

Chrétien, J. (1990) 'L'ethnisme au Burundi: tragédies et propagandes', *Politique Africaine*, 39, October.

— (2000) 'Le Burundi après la

signature de l'Accord d'Arusha', *Politique Africaine*, 80b, December.

Clark, G. (2001) 'Gender and profiteering: Ghana's market women as devoted mothers and "human vampire bats"', in Dorothy Hodgson and Sheryl McCurdy (eds), *'Wicked' Women and the Reconfiguration of Gender in Africa*, Portsmouth, NH: Heinemann.

Collier, P. (2003) *Breaking the Conflict Trap. Civil War and Development Policy*, Washington, DC: World Bank/Oxford University Press.

Collier, P. and A. Hoeffler (2001) *Greed and Grievance in Civil War*, Policy Research Working Paper no. 2355, Washington, DC: World Bank.

Correia, M. C. and I. Bannon (2006) 'Gender and its discontents: moving to menstreaming development', in *The Other Half of Gender*, Washington, DC: World Bank.

Dexter, T. and P. Ntahombaye (2005) *The Role of Informal Justice Systems in Fostering the Rule of Law in Post-Conflict Situations: The Case of Burundi*, Geneva: Henry Dunant Centre for Humanitarian Dialogue.

Donini, A., L. Minear, I. Smillie, T. van Baarda and A. C. Welsch (2005) *Mapping the Security Environment. Understanding the perceptions of local communities, peace support organizations and external aid agencies*, Medford, MA: Feinstein International Famine Center, June.

Donnelly, J. (1989) *Universal Human Rights: In Theory and Practice*, Ithaca, NJ: Cornell University.

Economist Intelligence Unit (2006) *Burundi Country Report*, London.

Enloe, C. (2005) *The Curious Feminist: Searching for Women in a New Age of Empire*, Berkeley: University of California Press.

Erdmann, G. and U. Engel (2007) 'Neopatrimonialism reconsidered: critical review and elaboration of an elusive concept', *Journal of Commonwealth and Comparative Studies*, 45(1), February.

FAST (2005) *Burundi. Semi-Annual Risk Assessment. May to October 2005*, Berne: Swisspeace.

— (2006) *Burundi. Semi-Annual Risk Assessment. November 2005 to May 2006*, Berne: Swisspeace.

Feltz, G. (1985) 'Histoire des mentalités et histoire des missions au Burundi, ca. 1880–1960', *History in Africa*, 12.

Galtung, J. (1996) 'Violence, peace, and peace research', *Journal of Peace Research*, 6(1).

Gasana, J. (2002) *Conflict Prevention, Management and Resolution in Burundi*, <unpan1.un.org/intradoc/groups/public/documents/CAFRAD/UNPAN009002.pdf>.

Giles, W. and J. Hyndman (2004) 'Introduction: gender and conflict in a global context', in *Sites of Violence: Gender and*

Conflict Zone, Berkeley: University of California Press.

Gordon, R. (1997) 'Saving failed states: sometimes a neocolonialist notion', *American University Journal of International Law and Policy*, 12(6).

Hagman, L. and Z. Nielson (2002) *A Framework for Lasting Disarmament, Demobilization, and Reintegration of Former Combatants in Crisis Situations*, IPA Workshop Report, New York.

Hamre, J. J. and G. R. Sullivan (2002) 'Toward post-conflict reconstruction', *Washington Quarterly*, Autumn.

Harrison, L. (2001) *Culture Matters: How Values Shape Human Progress*, New York: Basic Books.

Hodgson, D. and S. McCurdy (2001) 'Introduction', in *'Wicked' Women and the Reconfiguration of Gender in Africa*, Portsmouth, NH: Heinemann.

Hoglund, K. (2005) 'Violence and the peace process in Sri Lanka', *Civil Wars*, 7(2), Summer.

Hyden, G. (2006) *African Politics in Comparative Perspective*, Cambridge: Cambridge University Press.

ICG (International Crisis Group) (2004) *Fin de transition au Burundi: franchir le cap*, ICG Africa Report no. 81, Brussels.

IDEA (2006) *Democracy, Conflict and Human Security: Pursuing Peace in the 21st Century*, vol. 1, Stockholm: International Institute for Democracy and Electoral Assistance, September,

<www.idea.int/publications/dchs/dchs_vol1.cfm>.

Jackson, T. (2000) *Equal Access to Education. A Peace Imperative for Burundi*, London: International Alert.

Jefremovas, V. (1991) 'Loose women, virtuous wives and timid virgins: gender and the control of resources in Rwanda', *Canadian Journal of African Studies*, 25(3).

Kaplan, R. D. (1994) 'The coming anarchy', *Atlantic Monthly*, February.

Karekezi, U., A. Nshimiyimana and B. Mutamba (2004) 'Localizing justice: Gacaca courts in post-genocide Rwanda', in Eric Stover and Harvey M. Weinstein (eds), *My Neighbor, My Enemy: Justice and Community in the Aftermath of Mass Atrocity*, Cambridge: Cambridge University Press.

King, G. and C. Murray (2001) 'Rethinking human security', *Political Science Quarterly*, 116(4), Winter.

Krause, K. (2004) 'The key to a powerful agenda, if properly delimited', *Security Dialogue*, 35(3).

Kritz, N. (1995) *Transitional Justice: How Emerging Democracies Reckon with Former Regimes*, Washington, DC: USIP Press.

Kwesiga, J. C. (2002) *Women's Access to Higher Education in Africa: Uganda's Experience*, Kampala: Fountain Publishers.

Laely, T. (1997) 'Peasants, local communities, and central

power in Burundi', *Journal of Modern African Studies*, 35(4).

Lancaster, P. (2005) *Report of the Independent Review of the Special Project for Child Soldier Demobilization, Social Reintegration and Recruitment Prevention in Burundi*, Prepared for MDRP, Washington, DC, October.

— (2006) *Categories and Illusions: Child Soldiers in Burundi*, Draft ms, Victoria: School of Child and Youth Care, University of Victoria.

Lawler, P. (1995) *A Question of Values: Johan Galtung's Peace Research*, Boulder, CO: Lynne Rienner.

Leaning, J. and S. Arie (2001) *Human Security: A Framework for Analysis in Settings of Crisis and Transition*, Working Paper Series, 11(8), Cambridge, MA: Harvard Center for Population and Development Studies.

Le Billon, P. (2005) 'Overcoming corruption in the wake of conflict', in *Global Corruption Report 2005*, London: Pluto Press.

Lemarchand, R. (1970) *Burundi and Rwanda*, London: Pall Mall.

— (1996) *Burundi. Ethnic Conflict and Genocide*, Washington, DC: Woodrow Wilson Center.

Louvain-Développement (2004) *Etude Baseline. Projet Lutte contre la Pauvreté au Nord Burundi. Situation de Référence Juillet 2004*, Bujumbura: Louvain-Développement.

Louw, A. (1997) 'Surviving the transition: trends and perceptions in crime', *Social Indicators Research*, 41.

Luttwak, E. N. (1999) 'Give war a chance', *Foreign Affairs*, 78(4), July/August.

McEvoy-Levy, S. (2001) 'Youth as social and political agents: issues in post-settlement peace building', Kroc Institute Occasional Paper no. 21, December.

Mac Ginty, R. (2006) *The Role of Accidental Spoilers*, Paper presented at a one-day conference on violence and ethnic conflict, Belfast: Queen's University, 12 May, <www.st-andrews. ac.uk/intrel/cpcs/papers/ Accidental%20spoilers.pdf>.

— (forthcoming) 'Post-accord crime', in John Darby (ed.), *Violence and Reconstruction*, South Bend, IN: University of Notre Dame Press.

Mack, A. (2004) 'A signifier of shared values', *Security Dialogue*, 35(3).

Malkki, L. H. (1995) *Purity and Exile: Violence, Memory, and National Cosmology among Hutu Refugees in Tanzania*, Chicago, IL: University of Chicago Press.

Mamdani, M. (1996) *Citizen and Subject: Contemporary Africa and the Legacy of Late Colonialism*, Princeton, NJ: Princeton University Press.

MINIPLAN (2006) 'Ministère de la Planification du développement et de la reconstruction nationale', *Enquête QUIBB 2006. Rapport final*, Bujumbura, June.

Minow, M. (1999) *Between Vengeance and Forgiveness: Facing History after Genocide and Mass Violence*, New York: Beacon Press.

Miyazawa, Y. (2005) 'Bougainville youth: their perception of peace and the peacebuilding process', *Peace Writes Newsletter*, 2005-2, Sydney: Center for Peace and Conflict Studies, University of Sydney, December.

Mungiu-Pippidi, A. (2006) 'Corruption: diagnosis and treatment', *Journal of Democracy*, 17(3).

Musisi, N. (2001) 'Gender and the cultural construction of "bad women" in the development of Kampala-Kibuga 1900–1962', in Dorothy Hodgson and Sheryl McCurdy (eds), *'Wicked' Women and the Reconfiguration of Gender in Africa*, Portsmouth, NH: Heinemann.

Ndarishikanye, B. (1998) 'La conscience historique des jeunes Burundais', *Cahiers d'études africaines*, 149.

Ndkimumana, L. (2005) 'Distributional conflict, the state and peace building in Burundi', *Round Table*, 94(381): 413–27.

Nduwumwami, D. (2006) *Document d'aide à la planification communale. A l'intention des membres du conseil communal*, Musaga.

Nkurunziza, J. D. and F. Ngaruko (2002) *Explaining Growth in Burundi: 1960–2000*, Working Paper Series no. 162, Berkeley, CA: Center for the Study of African Economies, <www.bepress.com/csae/paper162>.

Observatoire Urbain (2006) *Rapport Intermédiaire*, Bujumbura, January.

Okeke, P. (2001) 'Negotiating social independence: the challenges of career pursuits for Igbo women in postcolonial Nigeria', in Dorothy Hodgson and Sheryl McCurdy (eds), *'Wicked' Women and the Reconfiguration of Gender in Africa*, Portsmouth, NH: Heinemann.

Ottaway, M. (2002) *International Actors in Post-Conflict Democracy Promotion*, Memo prepared for the Conference on Democratization after War, Providence, RI: Brown University.

Paris, R. (2002) 'International peacebuilding and the *mission civilisatrice*', *Review of International Studies*, 28(4), October.

— (2004) *At War's End: Building Peace after Civil Conflict*, Cambridge: Cambridge University Press.

— (2005) 'Towards more effective peacebuilding: a conversation with Roland Paris', Interview conducted by Alina Rocha Menocal and Kate Kilpatrick, *Development in Practice*, 15(6), November.

Parpart, J. (2001) '"Wicked women" and "respectable ladies": reconfiguring gender on the Zambian copperbelt, 1936–1964', in Dorothy Hodgson and Sheryl McCurdy (eds),

'Wicked' Women and the Recon-figuration of Gender in Africa, Portsmouth, NH: Heinemann.

PBC (Peace Building Commission) (2006) Conference Room Paper for the Country Specific Meeting on Burundi, PBC/2/BUR/CRP.2, October.

Peters, K., P. Richards and K. Vlas-senroot (2003) What Happens to Youth during and after Wars? A Preliminary Review of Litera-ture on Africa and an Assess-ment of the Debate, Working Paper, The Hague: Netherlands Development Assistance Re-search Council, October.

Pouligny, B. (2006) Peace Opera-tions Seen from Below. UN Mis-sions and Local People, West Hartford, CT: Kumarian Press.

Pritchett, L. and M. Woolcock (2004) 'When the solution is the problem: arraying the dis-array in development', World Development, 32(2).

Prunier, G. (1994) Burundi: A Manageable Crisis?, Writenet, October, <www.grandslacs.net/doc/2505.pdf>.

Quinn Patton, M. (2002) Qualita-tive Research Methods and Evaluation, London: Sage Publications.

Rajasingham-Senanyake, D. (2001) 'Ambivalent empowerment: the tragedy of Tamil Women in conflict', in Rita Manchanda (ed.), Women, War and Peace in South Asia, London: Sage Publications.

République du Burundi. Minis-tères de la Planification du

Développement et Recon-struction, de l'Intérieur et de la Sécurité Publique (2001) Province de Ngozi. Plan Triennal de Développement Socio-Economique 2002–2004, Ngozi: PNUD/UNOPS.

— (2002) Identification des problèmes humanitaires et des besoins socio-economiques des ménages dans les sites de déeplacés, vol. 1, Bujumbura: UNICEF/OCHA/PNUD.

Reyntjens, F. (1995) Burundi. Breaking the cycle of violence, London: Minority Rights Group International.

Richards, P. (2006) 'Young men and gender in war and postwar reconstruction: some compara-tive findings from Liberia and Sierra Leone', in Ian Bannon and Maria Correia (eds), The Other Half of Gender: Men's Issues in Development, Wash-ington, DC: World Bank.

Richards, P. et al. (2003) Where Have All the Young People Gone? Transitioning Ex-Combatants towards Community Recon-struction after the War in Sierra Leone, Case Study 30, November.

Sall, E. (2000) 'Introduction', in Ebrima Sall (ed.), Women in Academia: Gender and Academic Freedom in Africa, Senegal: Council for the Development of Social Science Research in Africa.

Samii, C. (2007) Revolutionary Mobilization in Burundi, New York: Columbia.

Shaw, M. (2002) *Crime and Policing in Post-Apartheid South Africa: Transforming under Fire*, Cape Town/Johannesburg: David Philip.

Silberschmidt, M. (2001) 'Disempowerment of men in rural and urban East Africa: implications for male identity and sexual behavior', *World Development*, 29(4).

Smith, D. (2007) *What is It? Corruption in Conflict and Post-Conflict Zones*, Paper presented at a Fletcher School conference on Corruption and Peacebuilding, Medford, MA, April, <http://fletcher.tufts.edu/corruption-conf/publications.html>.

Sommers, M. (2005) *'It Always Rains in the Same Place First.' Geographic Favoritism in Rural Burundi*, Africa Program Issue Briefing no. 1, Washington, DC: Woodrow Wilson Center for Scholars, July, <www.wilsoncenter.org/topics/docs/IB001.pdf>.

— (2006a) 'Fearing Africa's young men: male youth, conflict, urbanization and the case of Rwanda', in Ian Bannon and Maria Correia (eds), *The Other Half of Gender: Men's Issues in Development*, Washington, DC: World Bank.

— (2006b) *Youth and Conflict. A Brief Review of Available Literature*, Washington, DC: USAID, EQUIP 3/Youth Trust, May.

— (2007) *Embracing the Margins. Working with Youth amidst War and Insecurity*, Paper delivered

at the Brookings Blum Roundtable, 4 August.

Stavrou, A., P. Burton, S. Johnson, K. Peters and S. Vincent (2003) *NCDDR. Ex-combatants 2003 Tracer Study*, Freetown: Multi-Donor Trust Fund.

Stewart, F. (2000) 'Crisis prevention: tacking horizontal inequalities', *Oxford Development Studies*, 28(3).

Sullivan, D. (2005) 'The missing pillars: a look at the failure of peace in Burundi through the lens of Arend Lijphart's consociational theory', *Journal of Modern African Studies*, 43(1).

Tamale, S. and J. Oloka-Onyango (2000) 'Bitches at the Academy', in Ebrima Sall (ed.), *Women in Academia: Gender and Academic Freedom in Africa*, Senegal: Council for the Development of Social Science Research in Africa.

Taouti-Cherif, R. (2006) *Beneficiary Assessment of the Social and Economic Status of the 'Child Soldier' Special Project Beneficiaries in Burundi*, Washington, DC: MDRP, June.

Taylor, G. (2006) *The Microfoundations of Civil War Participation*, Unpublished ms, New York: New York University, November.

Taylor, G., C. Samii and E. Mvukiyehe (2006) *Wartime and Post-Conflict Experiences in Burundi: An Individual Level Survey*, Paper presented at the APSA Conference, Columbia University, September.

Teitel, R. (2003) 'Human rights in

transition: transitional justice genealogy', *Harvard Human Rights Journal*, 16(69).

Tezare, K., T. Said, D. Baheta, H. W. Tewolde and A. Melles (2006) *The Role of the Eritrean Diaspora in Peacebuilding and Development: Challenges and Opportunities*, Toronto: Selam Peacebuilding Network, October.

Theidon, K. (2007) 'Transitional subjects: the disarmament, demobilization and reintegration of former combatants in Colombia', *International Journal of Transitional Justice*, 1.

Thomas, C. (2004) 'A bridge between the interconnected challenges facing the world', *Security Dialogue*, 35(3).

Trouwborst, A. A. (1962) 'Le Burundi', in M. d'Hertefelt, A. A. Trouwborst and J. H. Scherer (eds), *Les anciens royaumes de la zone inter-lacustre méridionale Rwanda, Burundi, Buha*, Tervuren: Musée Royal de l'Afrique Centrale.

Turner, S. (2004) 'Angry young men in camps: gender, age and class relations among Burundian refugees in Tanzania', in Philomena Essed, Georg Frerks and Joke Schrijvers (eds), *Refugees and the Transformation of Societies. Agency, Policies, Ethics and Politics*, London: Berghahn Books.

UN (2004) *The Rule of Law and Transitional Justice in Conflict and Post-Conflict Societies*,

UN Secretary-General Doc. S/2004/616, August.

UN Security Council (2005) *Report of the Assessment Mission on the Establishment of an International Judicial Commission of Inquiry for Burundi*, UN Doc. S/2005/158, March.

UNDP (2006a) *Monographie de la commune Busiga/Ruhororo/ Nyanza-Lac. Année de référ-ence 2005*, Bujumbura: Projet d'Appui à la Planification Locale et au Renforcement des Capacités des Communautés, April.

UNDP (2006b) *Youth and Violent Conflict. Society and Development in Crisis?*, New York: UNDP.

UNESCO (2000) *World Education Report 2000: The Right to Edu-cation*, Paris: UNESCO.

Urdal, H. (2004) *The Devil in the Demographics: The Effect of Youth Bulges on Domestic Armed Conflict, 1950–2000*, World Bank Social Development Papers: Conflict Prevention & Reconstruction Paper no. 14, Washington, DC.

Uvin, P. (1998) *Aiding Violence. The Development Enterprise in Rwanda*, West Hartford, CT: Kumarian Press.

— (1999) 'Mass violence in Burundi and Rwanda: different paths to similar outcomes', *Comparative Politics*, 35(2), April.

— (2003) 'Global dreams and local anger: from structural to acute violence in a globalizing world', in M.-A. Tetreault, R. A. Denemark, K. P. Thomas and K. Burch (eds), *Rethinking Global Political Economy: Emerging Issues, Unfolding Odysseys*, London: Routledge.

— (2004) *Development and Human Rights*, West Hartford, CT: Kumarian Press.

— (2007a) 'Development and security: genealogy and typology of an evolving international policy area', in H. G. Brauch et al. (eds), *Globalisation and Environmental Challenges: Reconceptualising Security in the 21st Century*, Berlin: Springer.

— (2007b) *Ex-Combatants in Burundi: Why They Joined, Why They Left, and How They Fared*, World Bank MDRP Paper, Washington, DC.

Vandeginste, S. (2006) 'Théorie consociative et partage du pouvoir en Afrique', in Filip Reyntjens and Stefan Marysse (eds), *L'Afrique des Grands Lacs, Annuaire 2005–2006*, Paris: L'Harmattan.

Weinstein, J. and M. Humphreys (2005) *Disentangling the Determinants of Successful Demobilization and Reintegration*, Washington, DC: Center for Global Development.

World Bank (2006) *Mission conjointe des partenaires du MDRP Rapport pays – Burundi. 20–22 septembre 2006*, Washington, DC: World Bank.

Yahya-Othman, S. (2000) 'Tanzania: engendering academic freedom', in Ebrima Sall (ed.), *Women in Academia: Gender and Academic Freedom in Africa*, Senegal: Council for the Development of Social Science Research in Africa.

Ziegler, J. (1971) *Le pouvoir africain. Eléments d'une sociologie politique de l'Afrique noire et de sa diaspora aux Amériques*, Paris: Editions du Seuil.

Index